Architecting CSS

The Programmer's Guide to Effective Style Sheets

Martine Dowden
Michael Dowden

Apress®

Architecting CSS

Martine Dowden
Brownsburg, IN, USA

Michael Dowden
Brownsburg, IN, USA

ISBN-13 (pbk): 978-1-4842-5749-4
https://doi.org/10.1007/978-1-4842-5750-0

ISBN-13 (electronic): 978-1-4842-5750-0

Managing Director, Apress Media LLC: Welmoed Spahr
Acquisitions Editor: Louise Corrigan
Development Editor: James Markham
Coordinating Editor: Nancy Chen

Cover designed by eStudioCalamar

Cover image designed by Freepik (www.freepik.com)

Distributed to the book trade worldwide by Springer Science+Business Media New York, 1 New York Plaza, New York, NY 10004. Phone 1-800-SPRINGER, fax (201) 348-4505, e-mail orders-ny@springer-sbm.com, or visit www.springeronline.com. Apress Media, LLC is a California LLC and the sole member (owner) is Springer Science + Business Media Finance Inc (SSBM Finance Inc). SSBM Finance Inc is a **Delaware** corporation.

For information on translations, please e-mail rights@apress.com, or visit http://www.apress.com/rights-permissions.

Apress titles may be purchased in bulk for academic, corporate, or promotional use. eBook versions and licenses are also available for most titles. For more information, reference our Print and eBook Bulk Sales web page at http://www.apress.com/bulk-sales.

Any source code or other supplementary material referenced by the author in this book is available to readers on GitHub via the book's product page, located at www.apress.com/9781484257494. For more detailed information, please visit http://www.apress.com/source-code.

Printed on acid-free paper

*This book is dedicated to all of the CSS professionals
who have ever been told they were "not real programmers."*

Table of Contents

About the Authors

Martine Dowden is the CTO of Andromeda, Founder and Lead Developer at FlexePark, and an international speaker. She focuses on web interfaces that are beautiful, functional, accessible, and usable, approaching user experience from both art and science, drawing from her degrees in psychology and visual communications. Martine is a 2019 Google Developer Expert in Web Technologies, a 2019 Microsoft MVP in Developer Technologies, and the author of *Programming Languages ABC++* and *Approachable Accessibility: Planning for Success*.

Michael Dowden is the CEO of Andromeda, Founder and Product Architect at FlexePark, an international speaker, a 2019 Google Developer Expert in Firebase, and a 2019 Microsoft MVP in Developer Technologies. For more than 20 years, he has been writing code and geeking out over technology. He is passionate about keeping things simple and focusing on what provides real value to the end user. Michael is the author of *Programming Languages ABC++* and *Approachable Accessibility: Planning for Success*.

About the Technical Reviewer

Phil Nash is a developer evangelist for Twilio and a Google Developer Expert. He's been in the web industry for more than 10 years building applications and integrating APIs with JavaScript and Ruby. He's British, but currently enjoying life in Melbourne, Australia. He can be found hanging out at meetups and conferences, playing with new technologies, or writing open source code. Phil tweets at @philnash, and you can find him elsewhere online at `https://philna.sh`.

Foreword

As an international community, the W3C starts with a mission statement: Web for All, Web on Everything. This means the Web is a medium designed to adapt to the needs and preferences of every user, and the constraints of every device. But that poses a problem for design. To quote the very first website:

"This implies no device-specific markup, or anything which requires control over fonts or colors, for example."[1]

In the early days of the Internet, web design seemed impossible. How could we have planned for every possible combination of user-needs and device capabilities into the future—from text-only terminals to smart speakers, watches, HD displays, and accessibility devices?

Nearly 30 years later, CSS is the standard web language of design, used on nearly every website and application we develop. But that broad use, and the low barriers to getting started, can lead us to underestimate this powerful language and the complex problems it is designed to solve.

As the web continues to grow its more important than ever for professional developers to understand how and why CSS works, and how we can get the most out of it.

In this book, Martine and Michael bring their experience and teaching expertise to the topic – leading us through every layer of the language: from cascade and inheritance, to progressive enhancement, web layout, responsive design, and architecture. This book is packed with guidance to keep your CSS resilient and organized.

Miriam Suzanne

---

[1] `http://info.cern.ch/hypertext/WWW/MarkUp/HTMLConstraints.html` (Retrieved 2020)

Miriam Suzanne *is a project manager, user-experience designer, and front-end architect. An accomplished writer and novelist, she authored "Jump Start Sass" and is a staff-writer for CSS Tricks (*`https://css-tricks.com/`*). Suzanne is a member of the Sass core team, and creator of popular open-source tools including Susy, True, and Herman. She is an Invited Expert with the W3C CSS Working Group and a teacher for the Mozilla Developer channel, producing resources for web professionals including tools, videos, articles, and demos. Suzanne is an international conference speaker and in 2017 she won the "Best Of" speaker award at CSS Dev Conference.*

Acknowledgments

Writing a book is a project of passion and commitment and takes a tremendous amount of time and support from friends and family, doubly so when writing multiple books in a single year. We would like to thank our children, Brook and Xander, for their patience during this process. And of course their grandparents, Marc and Elisabeth Ebtinger, for making it possible for us to dedicate time to writing and conferences.

Without the support of the technology and speaking community, we would not be where we are today. Lee Brandt and Kevin Miller were instrumental in getting Martine to start speaking at conferences. Along with Lee, Jeff Strauss and Jon Mills helped us expand our conference presence and meet a large number of other generous people. Nate Taylor prompted Michael to start speaking about CSS. Michael first met Chris DeMars because of CSS and Chris later nominated us for the GDE, which was significantly helpful. And of course we must mention Philip Japikse, fellow speaker and Apress author, who has been tremendously supportive and without whom this book would not have happened.

Many of those who influenced us on CSS are already mentioned within the pages of this book, but it's important to note the early and long-lasting influence that Dave Shea and Molly Holzschlag have had on our understanding of CSS.

Finally, we must mention those who contributed directly to the pages you're about to read. The Apress team of Louise Corrigan, Nancy Chen, and Phil Nash has been supportive the whole way, from walking through the proposal process to ensuring the quality of the finished book. Our last thanks goes to the many people who went above and beyond to support our research on the history of accessibility and the people involved, including Sarah Bourne, Fred de Villamil, Jon Baggaley, Andy Budd, Eric Meyer, Steven Pemberton, Dylan Wilbanks, Chris Wilson, and Chris Lilley.

CHAPTER 1

Cascading Style Sheets

This book on Cascading Style Sheets (CSS) takes a very different approach from most. It isn't trying to teach you how to design web pages and, aside from a cursory overview, isn't focused on teaching you how to use CSS. This chapter introduces the focus of this book, which is how (and why) to treat CSS as a programming language.

Classification

Cascading Style Sheets (CSS) are a web technology that allows layout, theme, and style to be applied to a document. In most common cases the document in question is a Hypertext Markup Language (HTML) file and the rendering is performed by a web browser.

Often CSS is seen as a design tool since it allows the author or designer of a web page to determine the visual look of that page. Because of its control over the final look of a web page, CSS has a direct impact on both usability and accessibility. Due to these factors, creating style sheets and writing CSS are sometimes assumed to be design tasks, and it may be the designer on a software team who is tasked with maintaining the style sheets.

It's interesting to note that before CSS became the dominant styling language of the Web, there were a number of other competing proposals. However,

> *"CSS had one feature that distinguished it from all the others: It took into account that on the Web, the style of a document couldn't be designed by either the author or the reader on their own, but that their wishes had to be combined, or cascaded, in some way; and, in fact, not just the reader's and the author's wishes, but also the capabilities of the display device and the browser."*[1]

---

[1]Bert Bos (December 17, 2016). A brief history of CSS until 2016. *WorldWideWeb Consortium.* Retrieved August 9, 2019, from `www.w3.org/Style/CSS20/history.html`

M. Dowden and M. Dowden, *Architecting CSS*, https://doi.org/10.1007/978-1-4842-5750-0_1

At its core, then, CSS puts control in the hands of both authors and readers. This makes it somewhat interactive and subjects it to the will of the reader of a web page, since they are able to influence the final look of a page based upon their own preferences. Most often when author intent meets the end-user influence to create a unique hybrid output, this is known as programming. So this begs the question: Exactly what *is* CSS? Should writing style sheets be considered programming, and should those who write CSS be considered programmers?

For starters, just like popular programming languages such as JavaScript and Python, CSS is a *language*. As shown in the "Structure" section, CSS has a specific syntax that must be followed and the rules you write cause actions to be performed. Additionally, the WorldWideWeb Consortium (W3C) refers to CSS as a language.[2]

One measure of a programming language is to ask if it is Turing complete. Skipping the formal definition, the simple explanation of a Turing complete language is one that can solve any arbitrary computation. Note that this isn't a strict requirement and there are some very useful programming languages that are not Turing complete, most notably Structured Query Language (SQL) and Regular Expressions (RegEx). However, if a language can be shown to be Turing complete, it should remove all doubt about its classification. The combination of CSS + HTML has received the formal proof necessary to be classified as Turing complete.[3]

This means that CSS + HTML meets the requirements for any general-purpose programming language, and that writing CSS and HTML counts as programming. This means that you are most definitely a programmer (or web developer, if you prefer).

Language Features

Despite the classification of CSS as a programming language, we can probably agree that using CSS + HTML for general programming tasks wouldn't be particularly convenient. That is because this really isn't the point of CSS (or HTML).

---

[2]WorldWideWeb Consortium. HTML & CSS. Retrieved July 30, 2019, from `www.w3.org/standards/webdesign/htmlcss`

[3]Lara Schenck (May 25, 2019). Is CSS Turing Complete? Retrieved July 31, 2019, from `https://notlaura.com/is-css-turing-complete/`

Regardless, there are many interesting features of the language that are similar to more traditional programming languages, including

- Variables

- Functions

- Calculations

- Imports

- Scope

- Comments

- Polymorphism

When utilizing CSS precompilers, you gain access to even more programming language features, such as

- Mixins

- Extension

- Namespaces

- List and map data structures

- Mathematical expressions

See Chapter 2 for a more in-depth exploration of the CSS language features and Chapter 7 for more on CSS precompilers.

Structure

It is important to note that CSS is a declarative language rather than an imperative one. This means that rather than writing code that tells a web browser how to apply styles to a page, we instead tell the browser what styles to apply and where to apply them. These declarations are called rulesets in the specification, but may be referred to simply as *rules*.

Each rule in CSS is comprised of one or more selectors and one or more declarations, as shown in Figure 1-1.

3

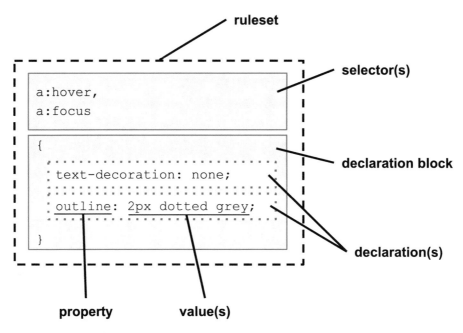

Figure 1-1. *CSS Ruleset*

Each declaration is made up of a property-value pair. As of this writing, the CSS Working Group listed 564 possible properties. Each property must be supported by the user agent (typically a web browser) for it to have any effect. Unsupported properties are simply ignored.

Rulesets may be further grouped and modified by at-rules such as `@media` or `@supports` and are collected into style sheets. A style sheet is simply a text file with a .css extension that contains any number of rules which describe the presentation of a document or web page.

Software Architecture

Once we accept that CSS has all the sophistication of a programming language, we need to accept the implication that we must treat style sheets like code. This means that we can take advantage of many principles, best practices, and design patterns of software architecture and apply them when writing CSS.

Note   You may find the term *software architecture* used interchangeably with the term *software design*. This is common within the industry and both terms refer to the same high-level design thinking and process methodology. Since CSS is often used for *visual design*, we chose the term *architecture* throughout this book to avoid any confusion between these concepts.

Software architecture looks at the structure and components of a system and weighs the pros and cons of various possible combinations and approaches. The strengths, weaknesses, and limitations of various systems and approaches should all be considered. The architect's approach is much more of the high-level bird's-eye view than a developer's (although often the same person will do both).

For example, if you wanted to animate an image moving across the page when a button is clicked, how would you implement that functionality? Would you use CSS or JavaScript? Would you use an <img> element, Scalable Vector Graphics (SVG), or Canvas? Which will yield the smoothest visual animation? Which approach will be the easiest to maintain when requirements change? These are the types of questions that software architecture attempts to evaluate.

You do not have to start from scratch when making these types of decisions. There are some well-established principles of software architecture and best practices that can guide you on your journey to more strategic decision making with regard to CSS.

Separation of Concerns

The term *separation of concerns* is credited to Edsger Dijkstra[4] and refers to the idea that it is very helpful for us to focus on one aspect of a problem at a time. As shown later in the "Web Architecture" section, a web application separates content, style, and actions and even uses different technologies for each of these concerns.

Looking at separation of concern as it pertains to CSS, what are some of the concerns we might find in a ruleset? As shown in Figure 1-2, we see that layout, theme, typography, and interaction are all aspects of a web page that can be controlled using CSS. See Figure 1-2.

---

[4]Dijkstra, Edsger W (August 30, 1974). On the role of scientific thought. Retrieved August 12, 2019, from www.cs.utexas.edu/users/EWD/transcriptions/EWD04xx/EWD447.html

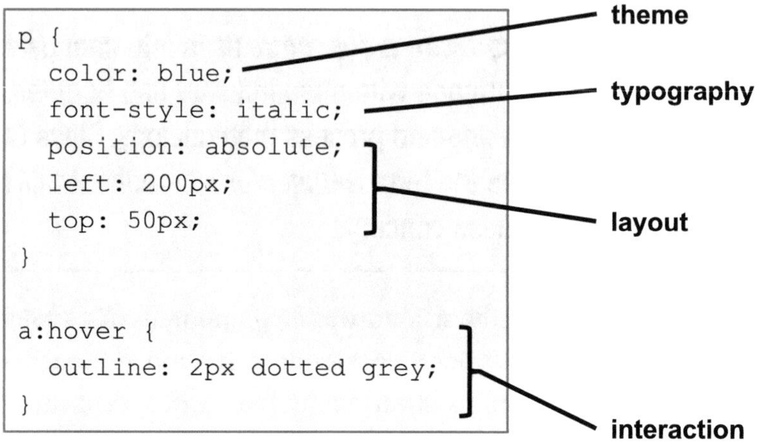

```
p {
    color: blue;
    font-style: italic;
    position: absolute;
    left: 200px;
    top: 50px;
}

a:hover {
    outline: 2px dotted grey;
}
```

theme

typography

layout

interaction

Figure 1-2. *CSS Areas of Concern*

Now, let's say you have a style sheet with 20,000 rulesets. This is clearly unmanageable and these rulesets need to be split into multiple files. How do you determine how many files you need and which rulesets go into each file? One approach is to split files based upon concern (e.g., layout vs. theme), while another approach would be to group rulesets based upon the specific components to which they apply. This question is quite fundamental to the discussion of different CSS architecture models in Chapter 10.

Two of the most widely accepted principles of software architecture, cohesion and coupling, serve to better define the idea of separation of concerns. These metrics were first published in *Structured Design*[5] and have since become standards in software engineering.

Cohesion

Cohesion can be described as a measure of responsibility. It is a qualitative measure of the breadth of different tasks or effects a given unit of code is responsible for and the nature of the relationship between those tasks or effects. Traditionally there are seven levels of cohesion ranked from *coincidental* (worst) to *functional* (best).

---

[5]W. P. Stevens, G. J. Myers and L. L. Constantine, "Structured Design," in *IBM Systems Journal*, vol. 13, no. 2, pp. 115-139, 1974. doi: 10.1147/sj.132.0115

Another popular principle that is related to cohesion is the *single responsibility principle* (SRP). The idea is that every function and module should have just one responsibility. There are two important goals that derive from this:

1. **Lack of side effects** – If a function does just one thing, then there is little risk of side effects or unintended consequences from its use.

2. **Only one reason to change** – Every time code changes, it increases the risk of introducing errors and bugs. If we reduce the number of changes, we can diminish risk. Additionally, this helps avoid side effects from system-wide change.

The goals of both cohesion and single responsibility are to promote simplicity and reduce risk, which are important goals for all of our architectural decisions.

Coupling

Coupling describes the interdependence between two or more units of code. Loose coupling is associated with good cohesion and generally describes a module with good reusability that may be updated independently of other modules with minimal impact on the overall system. This is an important attribute of robust and flexible systems.

Tight coupling is associated with poor cohesion and describes modules that are hard to test or modify independently. Such modules generally cannot be reused freely and may require larger testing efforts when changed. Favor looser coupling whenever possible.

When building web applications, we will find a lot of value in decreasing the coupling between content and design. Ideally we should be able to create style sheets that work for a wide range of content without adjustment. When we achieve this, we may say we have orthogonality.

Orthogonality

While an important and common term when discussing system design, the word orthogonality has accumulated some disfavor in recent years. This is likely due to a combination of misuse and poor definitions leading to it sometimes being described as "technobabble."[6] However, orthogonality is an important concept that is directly related[7] to cohesion and coupling, and it will factor into many decisions we discuss later in this book.

Orthogonality describes a relationship that is cooperative without being codependent, where two things work together toward a common goal while maintaining a level of independence.

In mathematics the simplest form of orthogonality of two vectors is when they are perpendicular to each other, meaning they form a right angle and intersect only once. Orthogonality can also be described as statistical independence, meaning two (or more) factors that vary without being influenced by one another

Taken into computer software, we use orthogonality to describe a relationship between two modules or components that are able to change independently of one another. For example, an HTML page may be considered orthogonal to its CSS if we're able to edit an HTML file to change the content and/or structure of the page with no corresponding change to the CSS, but the visual design of the page remains unaffected after the change.

In fact, this separation of concerns between document layout and structure is one of the original design considerations behind CSS.

Nontechnical Factors

In order to exercise separation of concerns, we must first practice the art of breaking down complex and challenging problems into simpler pieces. Often we find that seemingly impossible tasks are simply large accumulations of a great many simple tasks. In learning to see the individual pieces, we now have the building blocks that we need to create solutions.

Beyond the technical aspects of software architecture, there are practical considerations that must weigh into our decisions.

---

[6]RationalWiki. (July 2, 2019). Technobabble. Retrieved July 30, 2019, from `https://rationalwiki.org/wiki/Technobabble`

[7]Coffin, J. (December 16, 2015). Cohesion and Coupling: Principles of Orthogonal, Object-Oriented Programming. Retrieved July 30, 2019 from `https://medium.com/@jasoncof/9bf1eb92a2e5`

Cost of Maintenance

It's easy to buy into the idea that the cheapest thing to build today is the best financial decision; however, the true cost of ownership of a software product must include the ongoing cost of maintenance in the calculation. Often the thing that is the cheapest to build may be the most expensive to maintain. Perhaps we can purchase an existing third-party library or template and pull in updates from them instead of building and maintaining ourselves?

Development Time

We're often working on tight deadlines in an ongoing effort to deliver value to our customers and produce revenue for our company. The total time and effort of an architectural decision is an important decision point as it may affect both cost and timeline. Sometimes it's worth taking a big hit initially to ramp up on a new approach that will be faster over time. Other times we need to acknowledge that going with things we're already familiar with is the best choice. But do consider that development time is very expensive, so sometimes a decision that seems trivial (shaving 10 seconds off page reload time during development) may pay dividends later (10 seconds x 100 times a day x 260 work days x 5 developers = 15 days a year in savings).

Developer Satisfaction

While the technical and financial impact of our decisions are relatively straightforward, the impact decisions can have on morale are just as important and easy to overlook. So when deciding between CSS, Sass, and Less or selecting your next CSS framework, the attitude and buy-in from your team is an important consideration. Sometimes the friction can be the usual resistance to change or the pace of change; sometimes it's a legitimate concern that the decision is not the best fit for the product or team. Yet other times it's because the developers don't feel the decisions are helping them build useful skills. Take these concerns seriously because morale affects performance, quality of life, and turnover.

Best Practices

It is important to acknowledge that the study of architecture revolves around defining solution patterns for common problems, but also that there is no absolute answer. No single approach is always right and no single decision will work in all cases. Practicing architecture is all about understanding your available options, weighing the positive and negative outcomes of each one, and then making a decision. Documenting these decisions, and the reasoning that went into them, is another important part of being an architect. It's essential that we – and others – can learn from both our successes and our failures.

There are a series of practices that are generally good defaults in decision making. Not that they are always the right answer, but that using them absent any compelling reason to the contrary will generally produce good results.

Don't Repeat Yourself

Often referred to as DRY, Don't Repeat Yourself indicates that duplication can be an antipattern. When a bit of code is duplicated ten times within a project, this means we must update ten places anytime this code changes. If we only update eight of these places in a future update, we may find that hard-to-diagnose bugs stick around long after we thought they had been fixed.

The same can be true for CSS – duplicating the same rulesets and declarations can lead to additional maintenance effort and inconsistency in appearance over time.

There are a number of available mechanisms to reduce duplication in our style sheets including cascading, inheritance, variables, and mixins.

Occam's Razor

The logical razor credited to Occam is: "Do not multiply entities without necessity!"[8] While Occam never wrote these exact words, this principle comes from his work on problem solving, making it relevant to a programming context. The principle of Occam's razor is perhaps better known as "the simplest working solution is likely the best one."

---

[8]Jonathan Schaffer (2015). What Not to Multiply Without Necessity, Australasian Journal of Philosophy, 93:4, 644–664, doi:10.1080/00048402.2014.992447

> **Note**   A logical razor is a rational principle used to shave off possible but unrealistic or unlikely explanations for a given phenomenon.[9]

Simplicity provides great value to our code. It can make code easier to debug, easier to read, and make it easier for new teammates to get up-to-speed. Also, this provides an excellent default barring any external factors – the simplest solution we can come up with should be sufficient for many cases.

You Ain't Gonna Need It

Sometimes referred to as YAGNI, the principle of You Ain't Gonna Need It is that we should generally avoid adding anything to our code that we don't have a specific requirement for. We should generally avoid premature optimization by keeping our code as simple as we can until there's a compelling reason to do otherwise. Often this even means ignoring the DRY principle until we know that we'll need a bit of code three to four times or more as the cost of minimizing duplication may be too expensive for just two to three cases.

Learn from Others

Use existing architectural patterns and approaches, such as those presented in Chapter 10. Use Google to find other people with similar challenges and learn from them. Take to social media to get help from colleagues.

Web Architecture

As previously mentioned, a web page typically consists of a document (HTML), style sheets (CSS), and possibly scripts (JavaScript), all provided to an end user through a user agent (web browser). The web browser performs a lot of activity to build the web page from these components. The Mozilla Firefox model is shown in Figure 1-3.

---

[9]https://rationalwiki.org/wiki/Logical_razor

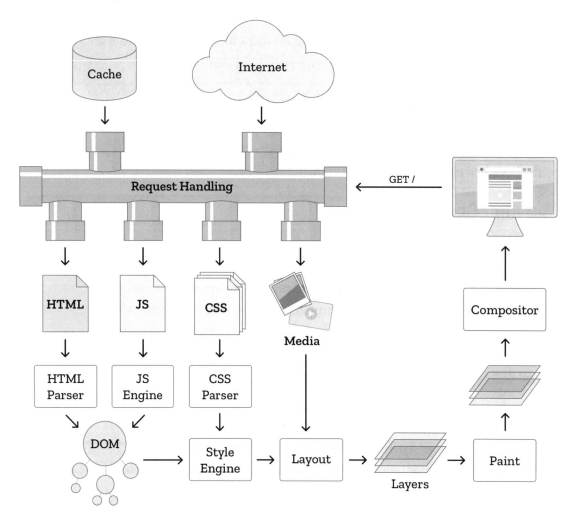

Figure 1-3. *Browser Engine*[10]

All of the source files must be retrieved from a web server, and then the text must be parsed according to its type. The HTML and JavaScript combine to build and manipulate the Document Object Model (DOM), which will be described in more detail in the following text. The Style Engine combines the DOM with the CSS to produce a layout, including any media files such as images or video. But even this layout is just a nonvisual model that must be rendered onto the screen using the paint and composition steps.

---

[10]Potch (May 9, 2017). Quantum Up Close: What is a browser engine? *Mozilla Hacks.*
Retrieved August 12, 2019, from `https://hacks.mozilla.org/2017/05/quantum-up-close-what-is-a-browser-engine/`

While it is not necessary to fully understand all of the activities undertaken by the browser, the relationship between HTML and CSS is of particular interest throughout this book. Since we've already covered an explanation of CSS, an overview of HTML and the DOM is provided in the following sections.

HTML

In order for CSS to work in a web context, the desired styles or style sheets must be referenced from the HTML (Hypertext Markup Language) document. There are three possible options, but the best method for most scenarios is going to be linking to an external style sheet file as shown in Listing 1-1.

Listing 1-1. Link to External Style Sheet

```
<!DOCTYPE>
<html>
<head>
  <title>Linked Style Sheet</title>
  <link rel="stylesheet" href="styles.css">
</head>
<body>
  <p>Sample HTML</p>
</body>
</html>
```

In some rare cases it may be necessary or desirable for the HTML to be self-contained and include all of the style information within a single file. This can be achieved using the style tag shown in Listing 1-2.

Listing 1-2. Self-Contained Styles

```
<!DOCTYPE>
<html>
<head>
  <title>Embedded Style Sheet</title>
  <style>
    p { font-weight: bold; }
  </style>
```

```
</head>
<body>
  <p>Sample HTML (in bold)</p>
</body>
</html>
```

The final method is to include styles directly inline on the HTML tag as shown in Listing 1-3. Using this method is functionally equivalent to setting element styles directly using JavaScript.

Listing 1-3. Inline Styles

```
<!DOCTYPE>
<html>
<head>
  <title>Inline Styles</title>
</head>
<body>
  <p style="color: red">Sample HTML (in red)</p>
</body>
</html>
```

There are a large number of CSS features that are simply not available using inline styles, including most of the at-rules. Additionally, this "breaks" cascading and inheritance, which is described in more depth in Chapter 3.

The fact that an HTML document must specify its own style sheets implies an authoritative relationship from the document to the style sheet. A style sheet does not get to specify what documents it belongs to, but it can specify selectors and conditions that determine the situations where rules get applied to a document, a concept which gets expanded upon in the following chapters.

Because of the relationship between CSS and HTML, it is important to understand the structure and vocabulary of HTML documents as outlined in Figure 1-4.

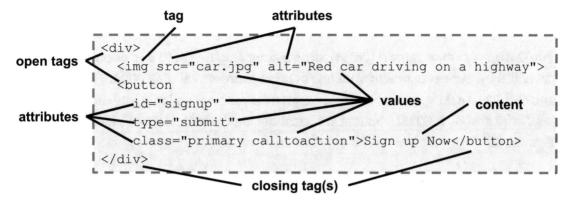

Figure 1-4. HTML Structure

As illustrated earlier, HTML is made up of tags which are demarcated by angle brackets. An HTML element refers to the entire content of a tag, from the first angle bracket of its opening tag to the last angle bracket of its closing tag. Some elements, such as <img>, have no body and thus no closing tag. Some elements, such as <div> or <button>, may contain text or even other tags between their open and closing tags. All tags may have attributes such as ID, class, or title. Some tags have mandatory attributes, which are required to be considered valid.

There are CSS selectors for tags, attributes, and values, which will be covered in detail in Chapter 2. One thing worth noting here is that some HTML tags exist primarily to provide semantic context.

Note   Semantics is the branch of linguistics and logic concerned with meaning. When applied to code, including HTML, we use the word "semantic" to indicate a word or tag that conveys a meaning or purpose beyond serving as a simple label.

For example, <div> can be used to group any arbitrary set of tags, but all this communicates is a generic division or grouping. The <nav> tag indicates navigation, <article> indicates independent and self-contained content, and <aside> indicates related but secondary content, much like the preceding **Note**. This additional meaning is helpful for user agents and screen readers, but can also be used within our CSS to write more robust and meaningful selectors.

Document Object Model

The Document Object Model (DOM) is the relationship tree built by a user agent which describes the entire document from one or more sources including HTML, JavaScript, and CSS. The DOM specification includes an API for access and manipulation by JavaScript and each HTML element and attribute map onto the DOM as illustrated in Figure 1-5.

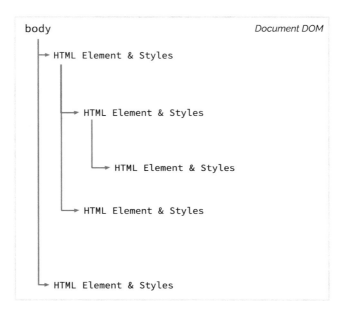

Figure 1-5. *Document Object Model*

Every item in the DOM is called a node. A node may be an element, attribute, or text, reflecting the underlying HTML. Also like HTML, elements have attributes. All of these can be read and modified directly using JavaScript for dynamic web pages.

Note that CSS doesn't factor into the DOM directly. However, it is possible to use the DOM to alter visual output by directly modifying the class or style attributes. Looking back at Figure 1-5, we see that the DOM provides the structure that the Style Engine applies the CSS to when producing a layout.

History of CSS

October Browser: WorldWideWeb, Tim Berners-Lee – first web browser	1990	
	1993	January 23 Browser: Mosaic – first browser to show with images inline with text
October 1 WorldWideWeb Consortium (W3C) Founded December 15 Browser: Netscape Navigator 1	1994	October 10 CSS first proposed by Håkon Wium Lie
August 16 Browser: Internet Explorer 1.0	1995	April 10 Browser: Opera 1
	1996	December 17 Cascading Style Sheets, level 1 (CSS1) Recommendation, W3C
May 12 A List Apart, Jeffrey Zeldman	1997	
August Web Standards Project (WaSP)	1998	May 12 Cascading Style Sheets, Level 2 (CSS2) W3C Recommendation
	1999	June 22 First 3 CSS3 Drafts: Color Profiles, Multi-column layout, and Paged Media

(continued)

April 14 CSS3 Introduction, W3C Working Draft	2000	
	2002	October 10 Wired News CSS Redesign[11]
January 7 Browser: Safari 1 May 7 CSS Zen Garden, Dave Shea	2003	February ESPN CSS Redesign[12]
	2004	November 9 Browser: Firefox 1.0
October Sass CSS preprocessor	2005	
	2007	July 4 CSS-Tricks, Chris Coyier
December 11 Browser: Google Chrome 1.0	2008	
	2009	August Less CSS preprocessor
April caniuse.com	2010	
	2011	June 7 Cascading Style Sheets, Level 2 Revision 1 (CSS 2.1), W3C Recommendation

(continued)

---

[11]www.holovaty.com/writing/136/ https://stopdesign.com/archive/2002/10/11/finally-
were-live.html

[12]https://mikeindustries.com/blog/archive/2003/06/espn-interview
www.holovaty.com/writing/192/

June 19 Media Queries, W3C Recommendation[13]	2012	
	2013	November 7 Style Attributes W3C Recommendation[14]
March 20 CSS Shapes Module Level 1 W3C Candidate Recommendation[15]	2014	
	2015	December 3 CSS Custom Properties for Cascading Variables W3C Candidate Recommendation[16]
March 1 CSS Flexible Box Layout Level 1, W3C Candidate Recommendation[17]	2016	September 29 CSS Grid Layout Module Level 1, W3C Candidate Recommendation[18]
September 25 Scrollbars Module Level 1, W3C First Public Draft[19]	2018	November 6 Selectors Level 3, W3C Recommendation[20]

(continued)

[13]www.w3.org/standards/history/css3-mediaqueries
[14]www.w3.org/standards/history/css-style-attr
[15]www.w3.org/standards/history/css-shapes-1
[16]www.w3.org/standards/history/css-variables-1
[17]www.w3.org/standards/history/css-flexbox-1
[18]www.w3.org/standards/history/css-grid-1
[19]www.w3.org/standards/history/css-scrollbars-1
[20]www.w3.org/standards/history/selectors-3

November 24		
Writing Modes Level 3	2019	
W3C Proposed Recommendation[21]		

Creation of CSS

Affecting the visual style of a web page was a known problem from the very beginning of the Web. Initially some basic visual controls were built into HTML, but problems with this approach were quickly identified. As mentioned at the beginning of the chapter, many people proposed, and even implemented, mechanisms for styling the Web, and during this time Håkon Wium Lie proposed the idea of CSS. Together with Bert Bos, he developed a proposal which was submitted to the newly formed W3C.

Lie and Bos went on to found the first W3C CSS Working Group along with Chris Wilson and Vidur Apparao, with Chris Lilley as the first WG Chair. The CSS level 1 recommendation was published 2 years later in 1996.

Dr. Håkon Wium Lie

In 1994 Håkon Wium Lie joined the WorldWideWeb project at CERN where he joined web pioneers Tim Berners-Lee and Robert Cailliau. In this first year, he drew upon his background in electronic publishing from the MIT Media Lab and produced the proposal for CSS. He went to work for W3C the following year, on the CSS Working Group.

Lie became the CTO of Opera Software in 1999, which was the most CSS-friendly browser at the time. He continued in that role until 2016 when the company was sold.

Dr. Bert Bos

While Håkon Wium Lie was working on his proposal for CSS, Bert Bos was producing his own stream-based style sheet proposal.[22] He reviewed the initial proposal for CSS and he and Lie determined that the two proposals could be combined. During the transition of the WorldWideWeb project out of CERN in 1995, Bos was hired to the newly formed W3C, where he continued working with Lie on the CSS1 specification.

---

[21]www.w3.org/standards/history/css-writing-modes-3

[22]http://web.archive.org/web/20000817100343/http://odur.let.rug.nl/~bert/
  stylesheets.html

Bos remains an active member of the CSS Working Group, having previously served as a chairman of the group. Together with Lie, he wrote *Cascading Style Sheets: Designing for the Web*, one of the very first books on CSS.

Chris Lilley

Chris Lilley started establishing web standards as a member of the Internet Engineering Task Force (IETF) working on HTML 2.0 and the PNG graphics format. He joined the W3C in 1996, initially working with graphics and fonts, chairing a Working Group on Web Fonts. When the CSS Working Group was formed a year later, he became the chair of this group. The following year he began 10 years as chair of the W3C Scalable Vector Graphics (SVG) Working Group. Over the years Lilley has authored and edited a large number of web and graphics specifications, and books on the same.

Chris Wilson

Chris Wilson was a founder of the first CSS Working Group and was credited by Håkon Wium Lie as the programmer who actually added CSS to Internet Explorer version 3, before the specification was even finished.[23] He has remained active in the W3C ever since, where he has held positions including chair of the Web Platform Incubation Group, chair of the HTML Working Group, and a member of the Advisory Board. He worked on Internet Explorer for Microsoft until 2009, and in 2010 he joined Google where he works on Chrome, specifically augmented and virtual reality capabilities.

Vidur Apparao

Vidur Apparao joined the initial CSS Working Group while working as Chief Architect at Netscape, where he was working on the Gecko Layout Engine. In addition to his work on the CSS group, he also contributed to the Document Object Model recommendations. After more than a decade as a web architect, Apparao has continued his career as a cloud software executive.

---

[23]https://dev.opera.com/articles/css-twenty-years-hakon/

Early Adoption

Before CSS was to become a well-known and proven technology, a few early web sites would need to take the plunge and update their old HTML3 web sites with inline styles to a more "pure" CSS-based layout and theme.

The first of these very public web site migrations was Wired News. On October 11, 2002, Wired News announced their redesign, including conformances to web standards and technologies including XHTML and an all-CSS layout. Eric Meyer had this to say:

> This new design is more accessible, faster to download, more flexible and much easier on the Web server itself. Anyone interested in the future of the Web need look no further than this.[24]

While Wired was making their big announcement, another team at ESPN was working hard on their new web site. Announced just 4 months later, their big victory was the (nearly) tableless layout.[25] By proving that building sites with CSS-based (instead of table-based) layouts could work for sites receiving millions of monthly pageviews,[26] these two web sites helped solidify the place of CSS as a powerful web standard.

Early Advocates

Without early advocates to inform and educate web developers, we might have a very different Web today. A large number of developers, including the authors of this book, were educated and inspired by these advocates, and this book does not stand alone but builds upon their years of work.

A List Apart

The very first major effort for web and CSS education and advocacy got its start as an e-mail list. A List Apart was founded in 1997 by Jeffrey Zeldman, who was soon joined by Eric Meyer. This early mailing list has grown into an entire ecosystem, including books and conferences, which continue to be influential to this day.

---

[24]www.holovaty.com/writing/136/

[25]www.holovaty.com/writing/192/

[26]https://stopdesign.com/archive/2002/10/11/finally-were-live.html

Jeffrey Zeldman

Jeffrey Zeldman started his career in web design in 1995, after a decade in advertising copywriting. The year after starting A List Apart, he cofounded the Web Standards Project (WaSP) along with George Olsen and Glenn Davis, starting a career-long push for open web standards. Zeldman was inducted into the SXSW Interactive Hall of Fame in 2012 and was the first person to ever receive the honor.[27]

Eric Meyer

Along with Håkon Wium Lie and Tim Boland, Meyer developed the very first test suite for CSS1 which was intended to help assess conformance to the standard. He joined WaSP the same year and cofounded its CSS Action Committee. Meyer has written six books on CSS along with countless articles for some of the most influential web design publications, including A List Apart. He also founded the css-discuss mailing list, and cofounded An Event Apart with Jeffrey Zeldman. In 2006 Meyer was inducted into the International Academy of Digital Arts and Sciences for his international work on HTML and CSS.

CSS Zen Garden

In 2003 a magical new web site was launched which demonstrated the power of CSS. CSS Zen Garden had a unique approach – it provided a fixed HTML document which designers were encouraged to style and theme as much as they wanted, using nothing but CSS (and images). By preventing edits to the HTML, web designers were forced to decouple their design implementations and the result was magical. The first few themes were provided by the site author, Dave Shea, but soon designers around the world were submitting their themes for consideration. This provided a powerful, hands-on lab that proved once and for all that CSS had a place as a first-class citizen of the web ecosystem.

In 2005 Dave collaborated with Molly Holzschlag to produce a book, *The Zen of CSS Design*, which sold over 70,000 copies and became the international standard for web design for some time.[28]

---

[27]www.austinchronicle.com/screens/2012-03-02/where-no-man-has-gone-before/
[28]http://daveshea.com/projects/zen-book/

Dave Shea

Shortly before launching the CSS Zen Garden, Dave Shea started a weblog about web design titled *mezzoblue*. For the next few years, he became a prolific blogger, providing valuable insights on a wide range of topics. Shea was active in the Web Standards Project as well as writing for A List Apart.[29]

Molly Holzschlag

While the Web was being conceived at CERN, Molly Holzschlag was launching her career in Internet technology. She published her first book on web design in 1996, going on to write more than 35 books on web technology and design. She has been widely recognized as one of the most influential women on the Web.

Holzschlag has worked directly with CERN, AOL, Microsoft, BBC, eBay, Opera, and Netscape to ensure browsers support modern standards. She has been project leader for WaSP, chair of the W3C CSS Accessibility Community Group, and a W3C invited expert to both the Internationalization Guidelines, Education & Outreach Working Group, and the HTML Working Group.[30]

CSS-Tricks

It is unlikely that anyone reading this book has performed a search for answers about CSS without coming across the CSS-Tricks web site created by Chris Coyier. For more than a decade, this web site has been sharing practical tips and tricks about CSS and other web development topics.

Chris Coyier

In 2007 Chris Coyier founded CSS-Tricks as a personal blog about CSS. Today the web site hosts articles from a large number of web developers and designers, including many listed in this chapter. Together with Tim Sabat and Alex Vazquez, Coyier founded CodePen, a very popular online code editor and sharing platform.[31]

---

[29]http://thewebahead.net/guest/dave-shea
[30]www.computerhope.com/people/molly_holzschlag.htm
[31]https://chriscoyier.net/

CSS Today

The CSS Working Group at the W3C is still going strong under fantastic leadership. The current modular approach to CSS level 3, along with a new trend of evergreen browsers, has led to a steady pace of progress. The following are a handful of active and influential people who, in addition to many of those already mentioned, are continuing to improve the state of CSS.

Rachel Andrew

Rachel Andrew is the author of more than 20 books about web development. She was a member of WaSP and is an invited expert to the W3C CSS Working Group. She is a Google Developer Expert, contributor to A List Apart, and the Editor in Chief of Smashing Magazine.[32]

Jen Simmons

Jen Simmons is a designer and advocate at Mozilla, where she works on Firefox specifically the Grid Inspector. She has spoken at many conferences, including An Event Apart and SXSW. Simmons is an active member of the W3C CSS Working Group where she has been extremely influential in the design and deployment of CSS grid layout. She has been an active web developer since 1998 and her clients have included CERN, the W3C, and Google.[33]

Nicole Sullivan

Nicole Sullivan is a popular speaker, with her conference appearances including An Event Apart and SXSW. She has coauthored two books on web performance and is an advocate for CSS and web standards. Sullivan started the Object-Oriented CSS (OOCSS) project which provides an architectural framework for CSS. Along with Nicholas Zakas she also created CSS Lint, a tool which helps catch common CSS errors.[34]

---

[32]https://rachelandrew.co.uk/
[33]https://aneventapart.com/speakers/jen-simmons
[34]https://aneventapart.com/speakers/nicole-sullivan

Miriam Suzanne

Miriam Suzanne is a project manager, user-experience designer, and front-end architect. An accomplished writer and novelist, she authored *Jump Start Sass* and is a staff-writer for CSS Tricks. Suzanne is a member of the Sass core team, and creator of popular open-source tools including Susy, True, and Herman. She is an Invited Expert with the W3C CSS Working Group and a teacher for the Mozilla Developer channel, producing resources for web professionals including tools, videos, articles, and demos. Suzanne is an international conference speaker and in 2017 she won the "Best Of" speaker award at CSS Dev Conference.[35]

Summary

In this chapter you've learned about the history of CSS, how it has developed into a programming language, and how CSS fits into the construction of a web page. Specifically, you've learned:

- The names of the various parts of a CSS ruleset

- That CSS is a programming language and why this is important

- How a user agent such as a web browser applies CSS to a web page

In the next chapter you will get a review of the basic CSS language features, with special attention to advanced and less commonly used language features.

---

[35]`www.miriamsuzanne.com/who/`

CHAPTER 2

Rules and Selectors

While you may already be familiar with the basics of CSS, this chapter provides a quick overview of the language features at your disposal when making architectural decisions. An important part of software architecture is having a deep understanding of the tools and methods available to accomplish various tasks to achieve our system goals.

Selectors

As we saw in Chapter 1, selectors are the part of a CSS ruleset that determine exactly which elements get style declarations applied. Proficient use of selectors can go a long way toward decoupling HTML and CSS making for robust and consistently styled web sites and web applications.

Basics

The basic selectors allow elements to be selected based upon their obvious qualities as rendered in HTML: tag names, attributes, and class names. The CSS selector syntax is so expressive that there is a DOM function `querySelector` which accepts a CSS selector string to locate elements in the DOM tree. See Chapter 8 for more about JavaScript.

Universal Selector

The * in CSS is a universal selector that matches every element on the page. Sometimes this can be helpful, such as Listing 2-1 and Figure 2-1, which adds a visible indicator to any element selected with the keyboard.

Listing 2-1. Outline Selected Elements

```
*:focus {
  outline: 1px dotted grey;
}
```

© Martine Dowden and Michael Dowden 2020
M. Dowden and M. Dowden, *Architecting CSS*, https://doi.org/10.1007/978-1-4842-5750-0_2

Figure 2-1. *Universal Selector*

However, this convenience comes at a cost – the universal selector effectively short-circuits inheritance for the associated declarations.

Unless you have a specific use case, it's generally best to avoid the universal selector in favor of inheritance. It's also a good idea to use the universal selector in combination with other selectors.

One use case for the universal selector is to apply a declaration to all children of another element, even if that property wouldn't be inherited, such as a border. For this use case, consider either custom properties or mixins as an alternative to this approach.

Type Selector

Selecting an element in CSS can be as simple as using the tag name. This is called the type selector, and all HTML tags are valid selectors.

The example in Listing 2-2 and Figure 2-2 adds padding to all paragraph elements.

Listing 2-2. Add Padding to Selected Elements

```
p {
  padding: 0.5rem;
}
```

Figure 2-2. *Type Selector*

Class Selector

To select an element by its class, simply use a dot followed by the class name, such as
.example. Since an HTML element can have multiple classes, multiple class selectors
may be combined, and they can also be combined with element selectors. See Listings 2-3
and 2-4. Output is shown in Figure 2-3.

Listing 2-3. Selector HTML

```
<body>
  <div>
    <p>Lorem Ipsum...</p>
    <img class="outline" src="image.png" alt="art">
    <button class="outline">Cancel</button>
    <button id="ok" class="outline bold">OK</button>
  </div>
</body>
```

Listing 2-4. Class Selector CSS

```
img {
  width: 200px;
}
button {
  background-color: lightblue;
}
```

```
button.outline {
  border: 1px solid green;
}
button.outline.bold {
  border: 5px solid darkgreen;
}
```

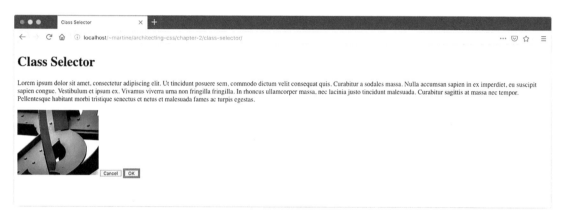

Figure 2-3. *Class Selector*

In this example, the `<img>` element does not receive a border due to the type selector. The OK button has a thicker, darker border than the Cancel button.

ID Selector

The ID selector # selects an element based upon its ID attribute. Note that the use of duplicate IDs on a single page is not valid for HTML, so this selector is expected to match either 0 or 1 elements. The example in Listing 2-5 uses the HTML from the previous example in Listing 2-3. Figure 2-4 illustrates the output.

Listing 2-5. ID Selector CSS

```
img {
  width: 200px;
}
```

```
#ok {
  font-size: 1.5rem;
  font-weight: bold;
}
p#ok {
  color: pink;
}
```

Figure 2-4. *ID Selector*

This will make the button text bold on the OK button. The example shows that the ID selector may be combined with type selectors in the same way as the class selector. By combining these selectors in a way that doesn't match the HTML, the contents of the paragraph tag will not become pink in this example.

Attribute Selector

The attribute selector matches an element based upon one of its attributes. This selector uses square brackets to contain the attribute match and may be optionally combined with a type selector. For example, a [rel] can be used to match all anchor tags with a provided relationship. To allow <area> tags to also match, use [rel] by itself.

In addition to testing for the presence of an attribute, this selector can test for specific values as shown in Listings 2-6 and 2-7 and Figure 2-5.

Listing 2-6. Attribute Selector HTML

```
<body>
  <h1>Attribute Selector</h1>
  <form>
    <button href="" title="go back">
      <i class="material-icons">arrow_back_ios</i>
      Previous
    </button>
    <label>
      Username
      <input type="text" >
    </label>
    <label>
      Password
      <input type="password" >
    </label>
    <label>
      Avatar
      <input type="file" accept="image/png">
    </label>
    <button href="" title="Continue">
    Next
    <i class="material-icons">arrow_forward_ios</i>
    </button>
  </form>
  <blockquote cite="w3.org">
    The World Wide Web Consortium (W3C) is an...
  </blockquote>
  <blockquote cite="https://en.wikipedia.org/wiki/Wikipedia">
    Wikipedia is a multilingual online encyclopedia...
  </blockquote>
  <a href="myfile.pdf" download>PDF File</a>
  <a href="myfile.docx" download>Word Doc</a>
</body>
```

Listing 2-7. Attribute Selector CSS

```css
label, input, a, button {
  display: block;
  margin-bottom: 1rem;
}
button {
  display: flex;
  align-items: center;
}

/* Matches password input fields */
input[type="password"] {
  color: red;
}

/* Strikes out any quotes cited from Wikipedia */
blockquote[cite*="wikipedia.org"] {
  text-decoration: line-through;
}

/* Underlines any element with a title attribute containing
   the word "continue" with any Capitalization.
*/
[title*="continue"] i {
  text-decoration: underline;
}

/* Display a gray border around any input which has an
   accept starting with image, such as image/png
*/
input[accept^="image"] {
  border: solid 4px gray;
}

/* Display a PDF icon beside any .pdf download links */
a[href$=".pdf"]::before {
  content: url(icon-pdf.png);
```

```
}

/* Matches a material design icon such as <i class="material-icons">arrow_
back_ios</i> */
i[class|="material-icons"] {
  color: blue;
  width: 32px;
}
```

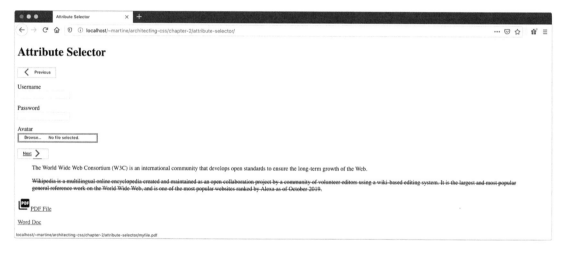

Figure 2-5. *Attribute Selector*

Because class and ID are both HTML attributes, the class and ID selectors have attribute selector equivalents, shown here in Table 2-1.

Table 2-1. *Attribute Selector Equivalents*

	Basic Selector	**Attribute Selector**
Select by ID	#contactForm	[id=contactForm]
Select by Class	.outline	[class~="outline"]

Grouping   To minimize duplication of declaration blocks, selectors can be grouped together into a comma-delimited list. For example, a, button { ... } would apply the declaration block to both anchor and button elements in the HTML.

Combinators

We've already seen how to combine type selectors with class and ID selectors, but what if we want to combine multiple type selectors or even attribute selectors? There are a few other combinators to make this possible, and they even provide for hierarchical context based upon the elements' relationship within the DOM. Examples of the combinators in Table 2-2 can be found in Listings 2-8 and 2-9 and Figure 2-6.

Table 2-2. *Combinators*

Name	Combinator	Example	Description
Descendant	" " (space)	nav a	All anchor tags inside of a nav element
Child	">"	nav > ul > li	First list items inside a navigation list, ignoring any items after the first level
Sibling	"~"	p ~ p	All paragraphs (after the first) that share the same parent element
Adjacent Sibling	"+"	h2 + p	All paragraphs that immediately follow an \<h2\> tag on the same hierarchy

Listing 2-8. Combinators HTML

```
<body>
  <h1>Combinators</h1>
  <nav>
    <ul>
      <li><a href="">Home</a></li>
      <li>
        <a href="">Combinators</a>
        <ul>
```

```
        <li>" " (space)</li>
        <li>&gt;</li>
        <li>~</li>
        <li>+</li>
      </ul>
    </li>
  </ul>
</nav>
<main>
  <h2>List of Combinators</h2>
  <p>There are a few other combinators to make this...</p>
  <ul>
    <li>
      " " (space)
      <ul>
        <li>nav li</li>
        <li>nav a</li>
      </ul>
    </li>
    <li>></li>
    <li>~</li>
    <li>+</li>
  </ul>
  <p>By combining selectors together we can select...</p>
</main>
</body>
```

Listing 2-9. Combinators CSS

```
nav a {
  display: block;
  margin: 0 1rem;
}

nav > ul > li {
  border: solid 1px gray;
  display: inline-block;
```

```
  list-style-type: none;
  vertical-align: top;
}

p ~ p {
  color: purple;
  font-weight: bold;
}

h2 + p {
  font-family: sans-serif;
}
```

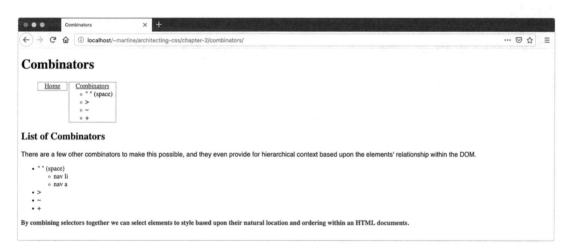

Figure 2-6. *Combinators*

By combining selectors together, we can select elements to style based upon their natural location and ordering within an HTML document. This can help us separate concerns between layout, theming, and content for more manageable rulesets.

Pseudo Elements

Pseudo elements allow you to select elements that do not exist within the HTML document, but show on the screen visually. Both `::first-letter` and `::first-line` select a portion of text within an element.

While the effect of ::first-letter could be reproduced by adding a <span> tag around the desired letters, for fluid layouts there is actually no other way to select the entire first line of a text block than ::first-line. This is because this rule is applied *after* the layout has been calculated so that the browser knows which words should be affected by the rule. See Listings 2-10 and 2-11 and Figure 2-7.

Listing 2-10. Pseudo Elements HTML – ::first-line and ::first-level

```
<body>
  <h1>Pseudo Elements</h1>
  <p>Lorem ipsum dolor sit amet, consectetur...</p>
  <p>Cras id blandit risus. Nunc dictum, elit...</p>
  <p>Quisque euismod tempus erat, sit amet pharetra...</p>
</body>
```

Listing 2-11. Pseudo Elements CSS – ::first-line and ::first-level

```
p::first-letter {
  color: red;
  font-size: 3rem;
  line-height: 0;
  display: block;
  float: left;
  margin-top: .125rem;
  margin-right: .5rem;
}

p::first-line {
  color: red;
}
```

Figure 2-7. *Pseudo Elements – ::first-line and ::first-level*

The ::after and ::before pseudo elements use the content property to insert content (either text or an image) based upon specific criteria. We see this in action in Listings 2-12 and 2-13 and Figure 2-8.

Listing 2-12. Pseudo Elements HTML – ::before and ::after

```
<body>
  <a href>First Link</a>
  <a href>Second Link</a>
  <a href>Third Link</a>
</body>
```

Listing 2-13. Pseudo Elements CSS – ::before and ::after

```
a {
  display: block;
}
a::before {
  content: url(link.png);
  display: inline-block;
  margin-right: .5rem;
  vertical-align: middle;
}
```

```
a::after {
  content: ' (link)'
}
```

Figure 2-8. *Pseudo Elements – ::before and ::after*

Have you ever wanted to customize the placeholder text on an input element? You can do that with input[type=text]::placeholder (see Listings 2-14 and 2-15 and Figures 2-9 and 2-10).

Listing 2-14. Pseudo Elements HTML – ::placeholder, ::selection, and ::backdrop

```
<form>
  <label>
    Username:
    <input type="text" placeholder="Example: user@email.com">
  </label>
</form>

<video width="100%" height="250" controls>
  <source src="" type="video/mp4">
</video>
```

Listing 2-15. Pseudo Elements CSS – ::placeholder, ::selection, and ::backdrop

```
input {
  box-sizing: border-box;
  border-radius: 4px;
  border: solid 1px gray;
  padding: .5rem 1rem;
  font-size: 1rem;
```

```
  width: 100%;
}
input[type=text]::placeholder {
  font-family: cursive;
}
::selection {
  background-color: cornflowerblue;
  color: white;
}

::backdrop {
  background: cornflowerblue;
}
```

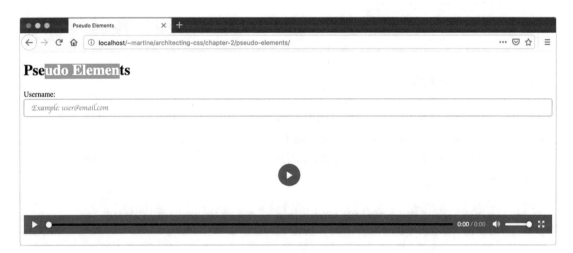

Figure 2-9. *Pseudo Elements – ::placeholder and ::selection*

Figure 2-10. *Pseudo Elements – ::backdrop*

Have you selected text on a web site and noticed that the selection highlight was in the site's brand colors? This can be accomplished with `*::selection {background-color: cornflowerblue}`.

The background in full-screen browsing mode can be customized using `::backdrop`. Both are also seen in the preceding example.

Note   The CSS specification calls for a two-colon prefix before a pseudo element, such as `::after`. However, most browsers support pseudo elements with just a single colon (`:after`) without throwing an error. It is likely that you will see this usage in the style sheets you encounter and it is important to understand why it works. In general, we recommend the standard two-colon prefix for two reasons: (1) it adheres to the CSS specification and (2) it clearly distinguishes pseudo elements from pseudo classes.

Pseudo Classes

Pseudo classes select elements based upon information that is not available in the HTML document. This may include state or context metadata.

Some of the pseudo classes make it possible to adjust styles based upon user interaction.

- `:hover` – Match when an element is being hovered over (such as using the mouse)

- `:focus` – Match an element selected with the keyboard (by tabbing), or with the mouse (by clicking the element)

- `:active` – Match an element in the process of being activated (such as clicking, while the mouse button is depressed)

- `:target` – Select an element that has an ID matching the URL's fragment (the portion after the #)

Displaying tabular data with beautiful formatting is made easy with the positional pseudo classes. Select the first and last rows of a table with `tr:first-of-type` and `tr:last-of-type`, respectively. Use the same technique to select the first and last columns using `<td>`. Highlight every other row using `tbody > tr:nth-child(even)`.

Managing forms and showing helpful indicators can use some of the following pseudo classes:

- `:in-range`, `:out-of-range` – Numeric value compared to defined range

- `:placeholder-shown` – If the placeholder text is currently visible

- `:invalid`, `:valid` – Checks the validation status of form fields for error and success indicators

- `:checked`, `:indeterminate` – Used to select a checkbox or radio button that is currently selected or if the selected option cannot be determined

- `:default` – Matches only if this element is the default in a group of elements (such as the default submit button or the default radio option on a form)

- `:disabled`, `:read-only`, `:read-write` – Matches the current status of a form field based on availability to user interaction

- `:optional`, `:required` – Matches fields based upon their required status

Another important pseudo class is the `:not()` selector, which select elements that do *not* match a list of selectors. While many of the pseudo classes have their inverse state defined (e.g., `:optional` vs. `:required`), there are many other scenarios where negation can be useful. For example, you can select every direct child tag of an `<article>` that is *not* an `<img>` by using `article > *:not(img) { ... }`.

Many of these pseudo classes provide capabilities to CSS that would otherwise require JavaScript involvement in designing the user experience. By leveraging CSS for context-sensitive UI implementation, we keep application and view logic separate, improving the maintainability and performance of our web sites and web applications. Examples of some of the previously mentioned pseudo classes can be found in Listings 2-16 and 2-17 illustrated in Figure 2-11.

Listing 2-16. Pseudo Classes HTML

```
<body>
  <h1>Pseudo Classes</h1>
  <table>
    <thead>
      <th>Name</th>
      <th>Email</th>
      <th>Zip Code</th>
    </thead>
    <tbody>
      <tr>
        <td>Jane</td>
        <td>jane@email.com</td>
        <td>15978</td>
      </tr>
      <tr>
        <td>John</td>
        <td>john@email.com</td>
        <td>11458</td>
      </tr>
      <tr>
        <td>Alex</td>
        <td>alex@email.com</td>
        <td>68978</td>
      </tr>
    </tbody>
  </table>
  <form>
    <label>
      Name:
      <input type="text" maxlength="20" required>
    </label>
    <label>
      Email
      <input type="email" maxlength="100" required>
```

```
    </label>
    <label>
      Zip Code:
      <input type="number" max="99999">
    </label>
    <button type="submit">Submit</button>
  </form>
</body>
```

Listing 2-17. Pseudo Classes CSS

```
table {
  border-collapse: collapse;
  margin-bottom: 1rem;;
  width: 100%;
}
tr {
  border-top: solid 1px lightgrey;
  border-bottom: solid 1px lightgrey;
}
tbody tr:nth-last-of-type(odd) {
  background: lightblue;
}
th, td {
  padding: .5rem 1rem;
  text-align: left;
}

form {
  margin-top: 2rem;
}
form > *:not(button) {
  border-radius: 4px;
  box-sizing: border-box;
  display: block;
```

```
}
label {
  margin-bottom: .5rem;
}
input {
  border: solid 1px lightblue;
  padding: .5rem 1rem;
  width: 100%;
}
input:hover, input:active {
  border-color: slategray;
}
input:invalid {
  border-left: solid 5px red;
}
input:valid {
  border-left: solid 5px green;
}

button {
  padding: .5rem 1.5rem;
  border: solid 1px lightblue;
  border-radius: 3px;
  background: white;
  margin-top: .5rem;
}
button:hover, button:active {
  outline: dotted 1px blue;
  outline-offset: 2px;
}
```

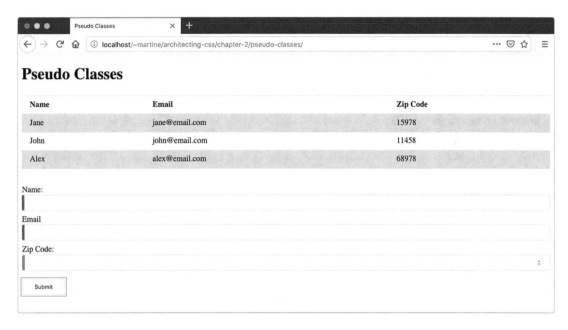

Figure 2-11. *Pseudo Classes*

Declarations

Selecting the elements doesn't do any good if we don't apply styles to those elements. The declarations section of each ruleset is where the individual style properties, and their values, are specified for the matching elements.

Properties

The properties in CSS refer to the various aspects of layout and style that can be affected. Many properties are available for some elements and not others. Sometimes the visibility of a property will depend upon the display setting of an element. For instance, the height property is ignored on elements with display: inline, but is rendered on display: inline-block.

Some of the CSS properties are a shorthand notation for a number of individual properties. Consider the example in Listing 2-18 where two declaration blocks produce the same results.

Listing 2-18. Border Property

```
p {
  border-width: 2px;
  border-style: solid;
  border-color: #666666;
}

p {
  border: 2px solid #666666;
}
```

Each of the individual border properties is available as an optional value parameter to the border shorthand property. Some of the other shorthand properties include `background`, `box-shadow`, `font`, `padding`, `margin`, and `outline`. Each of these has a different list of properties they summarize, and they have a specific order in which the properties should be provided. Be sure to check a reference when using these until you become comfortable with the syntax of each.

Some property and value combinations may produce results that seem similar but are actually quite different. Table 2-3 lists a few of these with an explanation on how they differ.

Table 2-3. *Property Disambiguation*

First Property	Second Property	Description
margin: 2px;	padding: px;	Margin is outside the box model and can be collapsed when adjacent. Padding is inside the box.
border: 2px solid black;	outline: 2px solid black;	Border adds to the box model dimension and exists between margin and padding. The outline exists outside the border and takes up no space on the box.
visibility: hidden;	display: none;	A hidden element still exists on the page and can take up space and receive events. An element that is not displayed effectively doesn't exist in the render tree.

The `outline` property is very useful for highlighting elements on the screen where you do not want the item to reflow. This is commonly used to highlight elements in combination with the `:focus` pseudo class. See Chapter 4 for details of the box model, as well as on properties related to layout, including `display`, `grid`, and `flex`.

A comprehensive review of the available CSS properties and values is outside of the scope of this book. For an excellent reference, we recommend the MDN CSS Reference from Mozilla, which can be found at `https://developer.mozilla.org/docs/Web/CSS/Reference`.

Units

There are a number of CSS properties that expect a `<length>` data type. This length is a scalar (numeric) value with an associated unit of measure. Selecting the correct units can make the difference between a nice fluid, responsive layout and one that breaks anytime the user resizes the window or zooms. The correct units can also have a tremendous impact on the amount of work it takes to achieve certain layouts.

There are three basic categories of units that we'll discuss. The first category includes absolute measures that are established at the time of the design. The second category is font-relative, meaning that if the user zooms the page or changes their default font size, the meaning of these values will change relative to one another. And the third category contains viewport-relative lengths, meaning they will change relative to the browser size or the specific display on the user's device.

Absolute

px – The traditional unit of measure for computer graphics; this is only suitable for screen-based displays.

in –Inch. `1in.` = `6pc` = `72pt` = `2.54cm`. This will be a true inch on printers, but defined relative to a *reference pixel* for screens which is `96px` regardless of the screen resolution.

pc – Pica. A traditional unit of measure in typography.

pt – Point. A traditional unit of measure in typography.

cm – Centimeter. 1cm = 10mm. See the earlier note on inches relating to printers and screens.

mm – Millimeter.

Note   Absolute units of measure do not scale relative to user settings such as `font-size`. As a result, the use of these units (especially on-screen) is likely to cause significant issues for accessibility and is not recommended.

Font-Relative

ch – Represents the width of the "0" character in the element's font (consisting of both typeface and size).

ex – Represents the height of the "x" character in the element's font (consisting of both typeface and size).

em – The calculated `font-size` of the element. If this unit is used on the `font-size` property, it will be relative to the inherited `font-size`.

rem – Exactly the same as em, but always relative to the `font-size` of the root element (which is the `<html>` for HTML documents). This is the preferred default unit for many web designers as it allows for manageable fluid layouts while addressing accessibility concerns.

Viewport-Relative

vh – Equal to 1% of the *height* of the viewport

vw – Equal to 1% of the *width* of the viewport

vmin – Equal to the *smaller* of vh or vw

vmax – Equal to the *larger* of vh or vw

Percentage

Many CSS properties will accept a `<percentage>` or a `<length-percentage>` (meaning either a length or a percentage). While the rem is the best choice for many purposes, especially those relating to content and accessibility, percentage works relative to any inherited size including font-relative, view-relative, or even absolute units.

Functions

While CSS does not allow user-defined functions, there are a large number of available functions to perform a variety of tasks, some of which are described as follows:

Shape – There are a number of nonrectangular shapes supported through the functions `circle()`, `ellipse()`, `inset()`, and `polygon()`. Combine with the `shape-outside` property to wrap text to a specific shape, or with `clip-path` to crop an image or container.

Transformation – There are a large number of transformation functions, including `rotateX()`, `scale()`, and `skewY()`. There are also 3D transformations such as `perspective()`, `matrix3d()`, and `scaleZ()`. These transformations can adjust the shape, orientation, and position of elements on the screen to create a wide range of visual effects and layouts.

Gradients – There are a large number of functions to support the creation of gradients, including `linear-gradient()`, `radial-gradient()`, `repeating-linear-gradient()`, and `repeating-radial-gradient()`. The blending of colors enabled by gradients supports a large number of visual effects.

Effects – There are other visual effects beyond just gradients. The `blur()` function will produce a Gaussian blur on the selected element, even an image. This can be useful for the backdrop of a modal dialog. The `drop-shadow()` adds some dimension to a theme. And `opacity()` allows elements to be somewhere between fully opaque and fully transparent, to allow dimensional overlays. (Note that if you want opaque text but a semitransparent background, you may want to consider using the `rgba()` or `hsla()` color functions as described in the following text.)

Color – The most common way of specifying color in CSS is with the 3- or 6-digit hex code preceded by a hash symbol, such as #FF0000 for the color red. Colors can also be specified by hue, saturation, and lightness using the `hsl()` and `hsla()` functions, or as RGB (red, green, blue) using `rgb()` or `rgba()`. The "a" in each of these function sets refers to the alpha channel which specifies level of opacity or transparency.

Colors can also be manipulated in a consistent fashion using the `filter` property with alterations such as `contrast()`, `saturate()`, and `hue-rotate()` and effects applied such as `grayscale()` or `sepia()`. These functions are particularly useful because they can apply to an image as well as text on the page.

Resources – The `url()` function is used to add image resources to a design through CSS. This allows the <img> tag in HTML to be reserved for images that are relevant to the content, rather than to the layout and design.

Counting – The counting functions `counter()`, `counters()`, and `symbols()` are used to manage counter variables. See more about counters in the following "Variables" section.

Math – Sometimes the built-in units aren't enough and you need to calculate size or position based upon other elements. The `calc()` function makes it possible to do some basic math with a mix of units. Addition, subtraction, multiplication, and division are supported along with parentheses. As an example, you could use `height: calc(10vh - 1rem)` to calculate the height of a header that was 10% of the viewport height, but accounted for a `1rem` border.

Listings 2-19 and 2-20 show the source code for Figure 2-12.

Listing 2-19. Functions HTML

```
<body>
  <h1>Functions</h1>
  <div class="shape"></div>
  <div class="shape"></div>
  <div class="shape"></div>
</body>
```

Listing 2-20. Functions CSS

```
.shape {
  clip-path: polygon(50% 0%, 61% 35%, 98% 35%, 68% 57%, 79% 91%, 50% 70%,
  21% 91%, 32% 57%, 2% 35%, 39% 35%);
  display: inline-block;
  position: relative;
  height: calc(100vw / 3);
  width: calc(100vw / 3);
}
.shape:nth-of-type(1) {
  background: rgba(255, 0, 255, 0.31);
  transform: rotate(-25deg);
  filter: saturate(15%);
}
.shape:nth-of-type(2) {
```

```
  background: rgb(255,116,0);
  background: linear-gradient(90deg, rgba(255,116,0,1) 0%,
  rgba(255,237,0,1) 47%, rgba(255,167,0,1) 100%);
  filter: opacity(.75);
  transform: translate(0, -50px);
  left: calc((100vw / 3) - 200px);
}
.shape:nth-of-type(3) {
  background: hsl(189, 100%, 50%);
  transform: rotate(25deg);
  opacity: .33;
  left: calc((100vw / 3) - 100px);
  top: -200px;
}
```

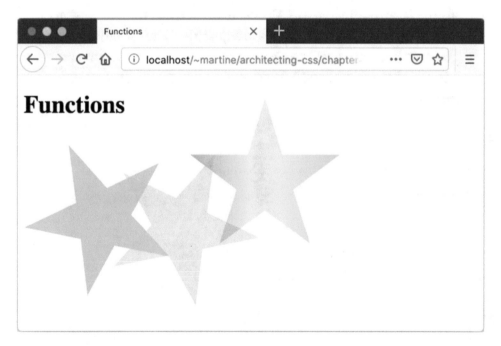

Figure 2-12. *Functions*

The example shown in Figure 2-12 highlights a number of functions. The position of the stars in the example is dependent upon the size of the browser window since calculations are based upon the vw and vh units.

Variables

There are a few ways to use dynamic data within CSS (examples found in Listings 2-21 and 2-22 and Figure 2-13):

> **Custom properties** – These variables are defined much like any other CSS property and can contain any value that would be legal in CSS. They can then be referenced later in a style sheet using the var() function.
>
> **Attributes** – Using the attr() function, you can pull in the value from an HTML attribute. Combine this with the content property to display attribute data in unique ways.
>
> **Counters** – Every HTML element can have 0 to many named counters associated within the document tree and manipulated using CSS. HTML lists generate a "list-item" counter automatically, incrementing by 1 with every list element unless explicitly reset. This also includes unordered lists. Use counter-set, counter-increment, or counter-decrement properties to adjust the counters and use counter() or counters() to display the value of a named counter in a way you choose. This exists to support nested lists, but may have many other uses.

Listing 2-21. Variables HTML

```
<body>
  <h1>Variables</h1>
  <ul>
    <li category="fruit">Apple</li>
    <li category="vegetable">Lettuce</li>
    <li category="starch">Corn</li>
  </ul>
</body>
```

Listing 2-22. Variables CSS

```
ul {
  counter-reset: li;
}
```

```css
li:before {
  content: counter(li)"-" attr(category)": ";
  counter-increment: li;

  text-transform: capitalize;
  background: lightblue;
  display: inline-block;
  padding: .5rem 1rem;
  border-radius: 25px;
  margin: 0 1rem 1rem 0;
}
```

Figure 2-13. *Variables*

At-Rules

The CSS at-rules (so-named because of the @ or "at" symbol in the name of each) are language features that provide some control over the structure of your styles. Among other things these rules provide a mechanism for collecting or grouping other rulesets.

@import

In Chapter 1 we looked at three ways to include CSS in an HTML document, including the `<link>` element. The `@import` at-rule provides a similar function for CSS. Both of these include pull mechanisms in a CSS file, effectively inserting its contents at the position of the import statement.

This is very useful as it allows us to break up style sheets into more logical and manageable files without any impact on the HTML document. See Chapter 7 for a more in-depth discussion of `@imports` along with other mechanisms for pulling in external style sheets.

@supports

The @supports at-rule allows rules to be applied based upon specific support of CSS features by the user agent. This is a way to provide styling and formatting based upon what a web browser declares support for, rather than using old-school hacks in an attempt to detect if a given rule will work as expected.

This at-rule allows you to start taking advantage of the very latest CSS today, by making it possible to provide alternate rules for cutting-edge browsers (or perhaps alternate rules for older browsers) such as in Listings 2-23 and 2-24.

Listing 2-23. At-Rules HTML

```
<body>
  <h1>At-Rules</h1>
  <p>Hello World</p>
</body>
```

Listing 2-24. At-Rules CSS

```
p {
  text-decoration: underline;
  text-underline-offset: 1rem;
}

@supports not (text-underline-offset: 1rem) {
  p {
    text-decoration: none;
    padding-bottom: 1rem;
    border-bottom: solid 3px orange;
    display: inline-block;
  }
}
```

Because text-underline-offset is supported by Firefox (Figure 2-14), Firefox ignores the @support not code. Opera, however, at the time of the writing of this book, does not support text-underline-offset and therefore uses the fallback code provided in the @supports not (Figure 2-15).

Figure 2-14. At-Rules, `text-underline-offset` Supported in Firefox

Figure 2-15. At-Rules, `text-underline-offset` Not Supported in Opera

@media

The CSS media at-rule is used to perform queries against the system, environment, or user agent. This use is called a **media query**.

Media Query   "Media Queries allow authors to test and query values or features of the user agent or display device, independent of the document being rendered. They are used in the CSS **@media** rule to conditionally apply styles to a document, and in various other contexts and languages, such as HTML and JavaScript."

—Media Queries Level 4[1]

These media queries can be used to build responsive layouts as discussed in Chapter 4, but they have many other uses. For example, a printer-friendly theme can be created that hides navigation and banners while retaining content as shown in Listing 2-25.

---

[1]Media Queries Level 4. (August 9, 2019). Retrieved from `www.w3.org/TR/mediaqueries-4/`

Listing 2-25. Printer-Friendly Design

```
@media print and monochrome {
  nav, .banner { display: none; }
}
```

Additional control over printing can be obtained by providing page-specific instructions using the @page at-rule.[2]

It's also possible to adjust the layout for devices that don't have a pointing device (such as a mouse) that supports hover, as is common with tablets and mobile devices. In Listing 2-26, we display the target URL beside every link, but only on devices that don't support hover.

Listing 2-26. Tablet-Friendly Icon

```
@media (not(hover)) {
  a::after {
    content: attr(href);
    font-size: x-small;
    position: absolute;
  }
}
```

Summary

This chapter covered the basic building blocks of CSS rulesets. You've learned how to

- Specify printer-specific layout and designs
- Insert document icons based upon the file extension using nothing but CSS
- Combine multiple selectors together into more advanced expressions
- Highlight alternating rows on a table
- Provide alternate styles based upon browser and device capabilities

The next chapter covers the *cascading* part of Cascading Style Sheets and demystifies the process by which a user agent decides the values of every property of every element on the page.

---

[2]https://developer.mozilla.org/en-US/docs/Web/CSS/@page

CHAPTER 3

Order of Importance

As mentioned in Chapter 1, one of the important features of CSS is the ability for the user, browser, and web developer to all exert influence over the final output of the page. The user agent, the author, and the user can all three influence the output of the page. To dictate what property value "wins," a multistep calculation is performed.

Inheritance

Inheritance is the mechanism by which CSS allows a value set on a parent element (such as <body>) to propagate to its descendants. This helps determine what value is used when no property is declared on an element property. The inherited value is determined by the computed value of a parent or ancestor. If none exists, the initial value, or default set by the browser, is used.

Not all property values are inherited by default.[1] Properties that do are generally related to theming such as typography-related properties (font-size, line-height, letter-spacing, etc.). Layout-related properties such as display, border, width, and height are generally not. If there is no declared value on a non-inheritable property, then the initial value is used. See Listings 3-1 and 3-2 and Figure 3-1.

Listing 3-1. Cascading and Inheritance HTML

```
<body>
  <h1>Inheritance</h1>

  <p>Lorem ipsum dolor sit amet, consectetur... </p>
  <img src="image.png" alt="art">
  <table>
```

---

[1]www.w3.org/TR/CSS22/propidx.html

© Martine Dowden and Michael Dowden 2020
M. Dowden and M. Dowden, *Architecting CSS*, https://doi.org/10.1007/978-1-4842-5750-0_3

```
    <tr>
      <th>Lorem Ipsum</th>
      <td>Lorem ipsum dolor sit amet, consectetur... </td>
    </tr>
    <tr>
      <th>Pellentesque</th>
      <td>Pellentesque sit amet massa auctor est... </td>
    </tr>
  </table>
  <p>Pellentesque sit amet massa... </p>
</body>
```

Listing 3-2. Cascading and Inheritance CSS

```
body {
  color: gray;
  padding: 2rem;
  text-align: justify;
  line-height: 1.5rem;
  font-family: Helvetica, Arial, sans-serif;
  font-weight: lighter;
}

h1 {
  color: slategray;
  font-family: 'Comic Sans MS';
  font-size: 2.5rem;
  letter-spacing: .0625rem;
}
h1 {
  font-family: fantasy;
}

p:first-of-type::first-letter {
  color: gold;
  display: block;
  float: left;
  font-size: 3rem;
  line-height: 0;
  margin: .5rem .5rem 0 0;
}
```

```
table {
  border-collapse: collapse;
}
tr {
  color: slategray;
  border-top: solid 1px lightsteelblue;
  border-bottom: solid 1px lightsteelblue;
}
td {
  padding: .5rem 1rem;
}

img {
  margin: 0 0 0 1rem;
  float: right;
  width: 200px;
}
```

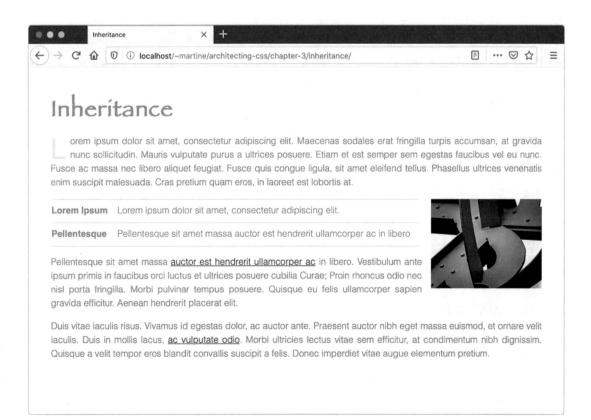

Figure 3-1. *Cascading and Inheritance*

The body attribute has a `text-align` property value of `justify`. Styles are not set on paragraph attributes; however, the paragraphs are in fact justified. The paragraph `text-align` value is inherited from the body's `text-align` property. Padding however is not inherited, which is why even though the body selector has a padding value of two rems, paragraphs, the image, links, and so on do not also have a 2rem padding value.

One of the main benefits of inheritance is that it prevents the need to write values for the same properties over and over again across different selectors helping with consistency of the styles and maintainability of the code.

In this example the color is also inherited, but the first letter of the first paragraph does not display in gray as set in the body selector, but in gold as set in the `p:first-of-type::first-letter` selector. The reason the first letter of the first paragraph is gold rather than gray is a question of specificity; `p:first-of-type::first-letter` is more specific than body.

Global Values

Inherit, unset, and initial are a little different from the rest of the property values available in CSS. These values are available on all properties and have the distinct difference of either resetting a value to default or to that of an ancestor rather than a new value. These values give you explicit control over how a property is inherited.

Examples for `inherit`, `unset,` and `initial` are based on the code found in Listings 3-3 and 3-4.

Listing 3-3. Exceptions HTML

```
<body>
  <h1>Exceptions</h1>

  <ol>
    <li>Cursive</li>
    <li>Unset</li>
    <li>Initial</li>
    <li>Inherit</li>
  </ol>

  <p>1 Lorem ipsum dolor sit amet, consectetur... </p>
  <p>2 Pellentesque sit amet massa auctor est... </p>
```

```
<p>3 Duis vitae iaculis risus. Vivamus id egestas... </p>
<p>4 Mauris vel mi quis lorem laoreet aliquet... </p>
</body>
```

Listing 3-4. Exceptions CSS

```
body {
  font-family: sans-serif;
  padding: 10px;
}

p {
  padding: 20px;
  border: dashed 1px gray;
}
p::first-letter {
  display: block;
  float: left;
  font-size: 3rem;
  color: red;
}
p:nth-of-type(2) { padding: unset }
p:nth-of-type(3) { padding: default }
p:nth-of-type(3) { padding: initial }
p:nth-of-type(4) { padding: inherit }

li { font-family: cursive; }
li:nth-of-type(2) { font-family: unset; }
li:nth-of-type(3) { font-family: initial; }
li:nth-of-type(4) { font-family: inherit; }
```

Unset

Unset works differently depending upon the property to which it is being assigned. If the value can be inherited from the parent, it will inherit; otherwise, it will set the property value to initial.

In the case of the list item, since font-family can be inherited, the second list item will have a font-family of sans-serif. The value is inherited from body, it's parent container (see Figure 3-2).

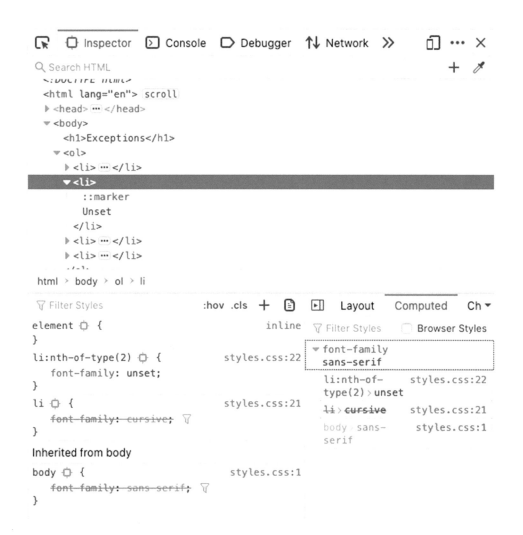

Figure 3-2. *Inherited Unset*

Because padding is not inheritable, padding gets set to 0 on the second paragraph tag because the initial padding value on a paragraph tag is 0 (see Figure 3-3).

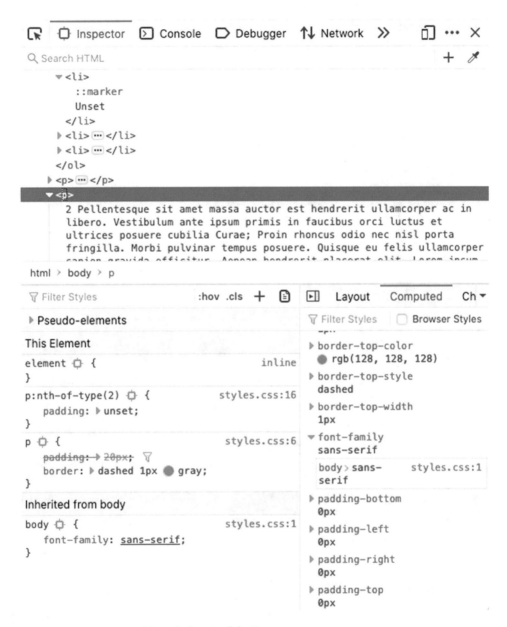

Figure 3-3. *Unset on a Non-inheritable Property*

Initial

The initial value for a property may be set by the browser and can vary depending on the user agent. If an initial value is declared in the CSS specification, then initial should return that value. Most modern browsers are consistent but mileage may vary.

For example, in Firefox the default value for font-family is serif. Therefore, the third list element font-family value is serif (see Figure 3-4).

Figure 3-4. *Initial*

Inherit

The property value will equate that of the parent's property whether the property is by default inherited or not. Padding is not inherited. Even so, when inherit is set on the padding property of the fourth paragraph tag, the paragraph tag takes the value set to its parent <body>. Body has a padding value of 10px; therefore, the paragraph also does. See Figure 3-5.

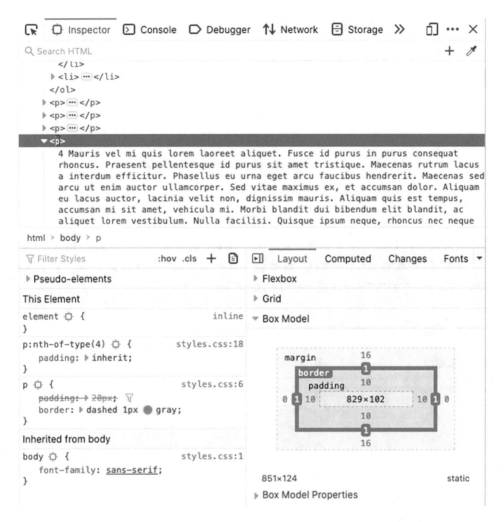

Figure 3-5. *Inherit*

As this example shows, we can force inheritance through the use of the `inherit` property, giving us direct control over the cascade.

Specificity

There is an order of importance given to the various types of selectors, based upon how specificity is calculated. There are four categories of importance summarized in Table 3-1, each of which is an order of magnitude more important than the one below it.

Table 3-1. *Selector Ranking*

Category	Selectors
A	ID selectors
B	Class selectors, attribute selectors, pseudo classes
C	Type selectors, pseudo elements
0	Universal selector

The specificity of any given selector is calculated as a three-digit number, with the digits A, B, and C, where A, B, and C represent the total number of selectors of their category.[2] Several examples are shown in Table 3-2.

Table 3-2. *Calculating Specificity*

Example Selector	A	B	C	Specificity
*	0	0	0	0
button	0	0	1	1
ul li	0	0	2	2
button:not([type=submit])	0	1	1	1 1
a[href$=".pdf"]::before	0	1	2	1 2
button.outline.bold	0	2	1	2 1
button#submit	1	0	1	1 0 1

Specificity plays an important role in determining which styles will get applied during the cascade.

---

[2]www.w3.org/TR/2018/REC-selectors-3-20181106/

Inline Styles   Styles applied directly to the element in the HTML such as

`<p style="margin-left: 10px">Lorem ipsum am met...</p>`

are inline styles. They are the equivalent of adding property values directly in the DOM with the use of JavaScript. Inline styles are given a specificity of [1 0 0 0],[3] which is higher than anything possible using normal selectors, as shown in Table 3-2. Inline styles are generally considered bad practice because they ignore inheritance and cascading. There are a few exceptions where they may be unavoidable though, including HTML e-mails.

Precedence

The order in which rules are applied matters. Directly targeted rules will always take precedence over rules which inherited from a parent or ancestor. If two rules with the same level of specificity are applied, the last one in order will be applied. This concept lies at the core of CSS and has since its inception, as indicated by its name "Cascading Style Sheets."

!important   The `!important` annotation is well known among CSS practitioners as both a powerful tool and a great liability. It's sometimes used by web developers to force a style to take effect when nothing else seems to work. But did you know that the *purpose* of `!important` is actually to improve accessibility? Because important user declarations always have the highest precedence, it gives the user the final say on which properties and values are set when the page is rendered.

As well as specificity, the source of the rule is also a factor in determining the value used by the element. Table 3-3 shows the order in which rules are applied during cascading, in order from least to most important.

---

[3]www.w3.org/TR/2018/REC-selectors-3-20181106/#specificity

Table 3-3. *Order of Cascading[4]*

Order	Origin	Importance	Precedence
1	User Agent	Normal	8
2	User	Normal	7
3	Author	Normal	6
4	Animations		5
5	Author	!important	4
6	User	!important	3
7	User Agent	!important	2
8	Transitions		1

In cascading, the last item to be applied wins; therefore, transitions will win over user agent !important containing rules over user !important rules and so forth.

Cascading

Cascading represents the way properties and values from a variety of sources, at varying levels of precedence and specificity, come together to determine the final set of styles that will be rendered.

It is important to note that it is properties that are cascaded to elements, not rulesets. The final state of an element may include properties that were declared in many different rulesets.

---

[4]Introducing the CSS Cascade: Cascading Order. *MDN web docs*. Retrieved December 5, 2019, from https://developer.mozilla.org/en-US/docs/Web/CSS/Cascade

To calculate the cascade, the following formula is applied:[5]

1. The declarations with the highest *precedence* are selected.

2. The remaining declarations with the highest *specificity* are selected.

3. When all other factors are equal, the declaration that appears *last* will be the one that is applied.

Value Processing

All of the different sources of property values are used together to determine the final value using the following calculation:[6]

1. First, all the **declared values** applied to an element are collected, for each property on each element. There may be 0 or many declared values applied to the element.

2. Cascading yields the **cascaded value**. There is at most one cascaded value per property per element.

3. Defaulting yields the **specified value**. Every element has exactly one specified value per property.

4. Resolving value dependencies yields the **computed value**. Every element has exactly one computed value per property.

5. Formatting the document yields the **used value**. An element only has a used value for a given property if that property applies to the element.

6. Finally, the used value is transformed to the **actual value** based on constraints of the display environment. As with the used value, there may or may not be an actual value for a given property on an element.

---

[5]CSS Cascading and Inheritance Level 3: Cascading. *W3C*. Retrieved December 5, 2019, from www.w3.org/TR/css-cascade-3/#cascading

[6]CSS Cascading and Inheritance Level 3: Value Processing. *W3C*. Retrieved December 5, 2019, from www.w3.org/TR/css-cascade-3/

This calculation from the W3C Specification references a variety of value classifications, which are defined as

- **Declared** – These are all the values (0–many) that match the element and property under review.

- **Cascaded** – This is the value (0–1) that is selected after processing the cascade.

- **Specified** – This is the value of the cascade, if available, or the default value for the property and element. There will always be exactly one (1) specified value for each property and element.

- **Computed** – The absolute value of the *specified* value which can then be inherited by child elements.

- **Used** – This is the final value that the user agent uses for the layout of the document.

- **Actual** – This is the value that is actually shown on a device, which may be adjusted from the *used* value due to device or environmental limitations.

The final actual values used for each property on each element are determined by a wide variety of factors external to your project code, including device, user agent or browser, user agent style sheet, and user-provided style sheet.

Summary

In this chapter you have learned the details of how CSS takes rulesets from many different sources and builds a cohesive set of applied styles for the web page. In particular, you've learned

- How HTML inline styles and !important annotations affect cascading

- How to calculate the specificity for any given selector

- The way properties are inherited within the DOM tree

In the following chapter, you will learn about the different options CSS provides for building fluid and responsive layouts that can adapt to variations in device and content.

CHAPTER 4

Layouts

Individual elements form a layout when they are put together on a page. Using CSS we rely on the box model to control the width and behavior of each element without the layout. To control how elements place themselves in relationship to each other, we can use properties such as display and float. In this chapter we define the box model and look at float, flex, inline-block, and grid for specific layouts.

Box Model

The base for laying out content is rooted in the **box model** which describes the rectangular boxes that are generated for elements in the document tree. As shown in Figure 4-1, the content is enveloped by three boxes: padding, border, and margin.

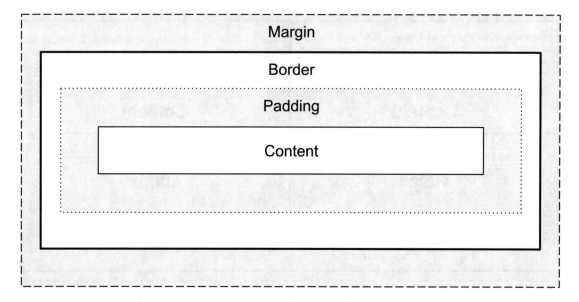

Figure 4-1. *Box Model*

© Martine Dowden and Michael Dowden 2020
M. Dowden and M. Dowden, *Architecting CSS*, https://doi.org/10.1007/978-1-4842-5750-0_4

Each of these properties, including the content, will be governed by dimension, type, positioning, relationship to other elements, and external information.

Box Sizing

Box-sizing, or the property that defines the height and width of an element, by default has a value of content-box which means that when a width and height is defined for an element, it is only applied to the content. Adding padding or margin to the element therefore increases the percentage width of the total available viewport that the element utilizes.

Content-Box

If a two-column layout, with each div equaling 50% of the width of the viewport, is desired, the amount of padding applied to each column needs to be subtracted from the width given to the element or the total width of both elements will exceed 100%.

Consider a viewport of 800px wide containing two divs. If no padding, margin, or border is added to the divs, and they are each given a width of 50%, their combined width will equal 100% of the viewport. If they are floated, they will sit perfectly side by side and take up 100% of the screen such as in Figure 4-2.

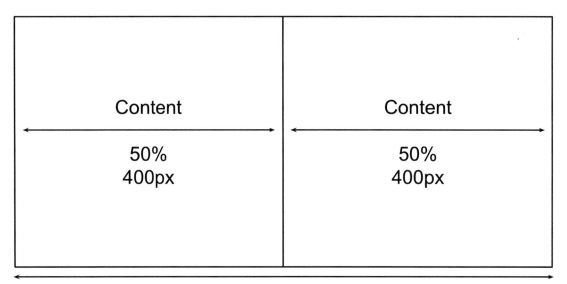

Figure 4-2. *Content-Box – No Padding*

If padding is added to the columns, the width of the columns will increase by the padding amount, causing them to exceed the width of the viewport. Figure 4-3 shows the columns with added padding.

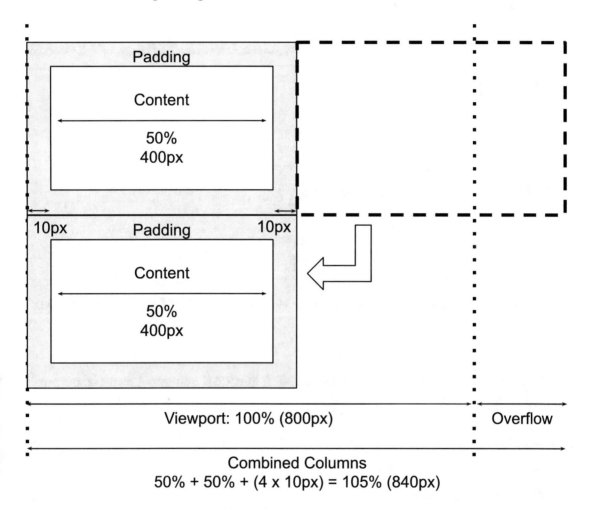

Figure 4-3. *Content-Box – With Padding*

If the divs are floated, the second would therefore be pushed below the first as their combined width is now greater than 100% of the container such as seen in Figure 4-4.

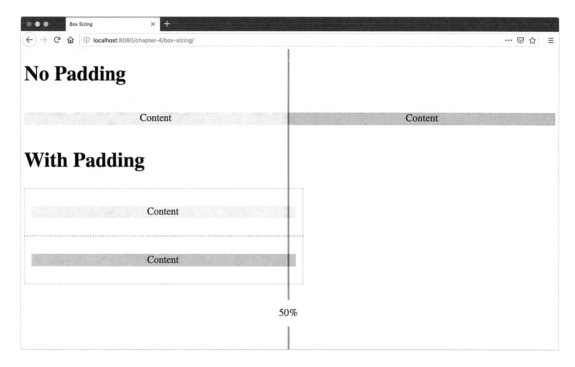

Figure 4-4. Effects of Padding and Border When Using `box-sizing: content-box`

In Code

Let's take the earlier described scenario and put it in code (Listings 4-1 and 4-2; output shown in Figure 4-4).

Listing 4-1. HTML

```
<body>
  <h1>No Padding</h1>
  <div class="container">
    <div>
      <p>Content</p>
    </div>
    <div>
      <p>Content</p>
    </div>
  </div>
```

```
  <h1>With Padding</h1>
  <div class="container has-padding">
    <div>
      <p>Content</p>
    </div>
    <div>
      <p>Content</p>
    </div>
  </div>
</body>
```

Listing 4-2. CSS

```css
.container { overflow:auto; }

.container > div {
  width: 50%;
  float: left;
}

.container p {
  background: rgba(0, 0, 0, .16); /* light grey */
  text-align: center;
}

.container > div:last-of-type p { /* second rectangle */
  background: rgba(0, 0, 0, .32); /* dark grey */
}

.has-padding > div {
  outline: dashed 1px rgba(0, 0, 0, .5);
  padding: 10px;
}
```

Border will behave the same way as padding; therefore, any border width applied will need to be included in the sum of content and padding to calculate the full width or height of the elements included in the layout.

Margin Collapse

Margins behave a little differently than padding. When sibling elements both have padding, padding from both is applied, and the space between the two elements is the sum of both sets of padding. Margin, however, depending on their context, can collapse. **Margin collapsing** is when **top** and **bottom** margins are combined or collapsed into a single margin equal to the largest of the margins applied such as in Figure 4-5 or, if all margins are negative, the size of the most negative margin. Left and right margins do not collapse.

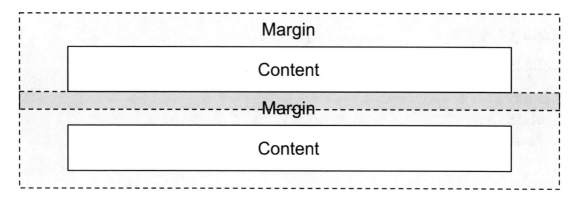

Figure 4-5. *Margin Collapsing*

Margins will collapse when

- There is nothing separating the margin of the parent and the margin of its child including padding, border, inline parts, block formatting context, or clearance property clear (e.g., `clear: right`, used with floats).

- Elements are adjacent siblings except if the latter needs to be cleared past floats (more about floats later in this chapter).

- Even when one of the margins is equal to 0.[1]

---

[1]Mastering Margin Collapsing. (August 4, 2019). Retrieved from `https://developer.mozilla.org/en-US/docs/Web/CSS/CSS_Box_Model/Mastering_margin_collapsing`

In Code

When two divs with 10 pixels worth of padding each are set side to side, they will only have 10 pixels of vertical margin between them (as seen in Listings 4-3, 4-4, and Figure 4-6).

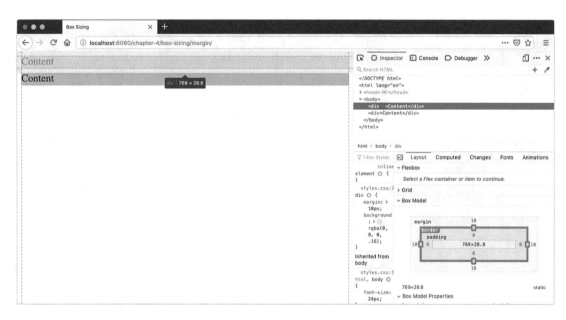

Figure 4-6. *Margin Collapse*

Listing 4-3. HTML

```
<body>
  <div>Content</div>
  <div>Content</div>
</body>
```

Listing 4-4. CSS

```
div {
 margin: 10px;
 background: rgba(0, 0, 0, .16); /* light grey */
}

div:last-of-type {
 background: rgba(0, 0, 0, .32); /* dark grey */
}
```

However, if we take the earlier example, where the columns have been floated and replace the padding for margin, notice that the margin does not collapse. The columns will still stack as their combined total width is greater than 100% [50 % + (2 x 10px)] x 2 = 105%, but because the divs are floated, the margins do not collapse. See Figure 4-7.

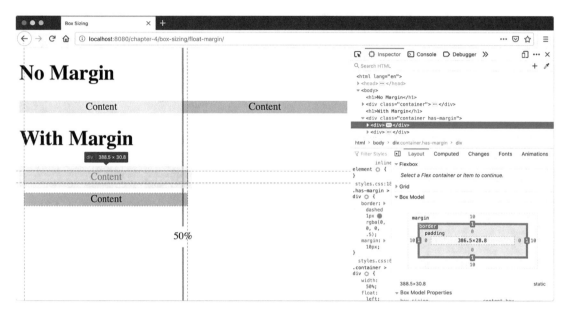

Figure 4-7. *Floated Divs – No Margin Collapse*

Unlike border, which can be applied to any element regardless of type, both margin and padding have restrictions as to which elements they can be applied to. Padding cannot be set on elements whose display property value is

- table-row-group(`<tbody>`)
- table-header-group (`<thead>`)
- table-footer-group (`<tfoot>`)
- table-row (`<tr>`)
- table-column-group
- table-column

Margin cannot be set on elements with table display types (e.g., `<tr>`, `<td>`, etc.) except table, inline-table, and table-caption.[2]

---

[2]8 Box Model. (August 4, 2019). Retrieved from `www.w3.org/TR/CSS22/box.html`

Pros and Cons

Although the mixins pixels and percentage-based values can lead to some interesting math, the benefit of keeping the box-sizing value as content-box is that when a width or height value is assigned to the content, it will not be subject to side effects from the padding added. The content will be exactly the height or width it was assigned by the developer. Furthermore, because it is the default value, the element's sizing will exhibit "normal" expected behavior without having to know anything about the other properties already set on the element.

Special Case: Outlines and Box Shadows   Outlines and box shadows, which create boxes around the border, could be thought of belonging to the box model. This is not the case because outlines and box shadows do not take up space. They overlay themselves, similarly to a position absolute as described in Figure 4-8.

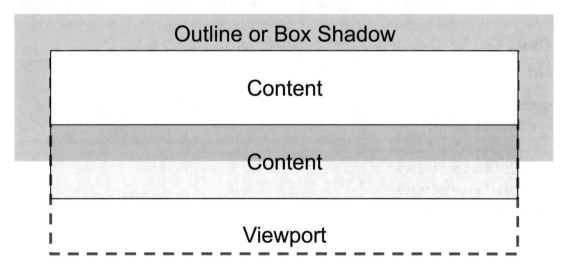

Figure 4-8. *Outline and Box Shadow*

The outline and box shadow not only overlap the content below but also bleed out of the viewport without the ability to scroll to it. Because they do not take up space, it does not constitute overflow, and the scroll bar is therefore not triggered. See Figure 4-9 and Listings 4-5 and 4-6.

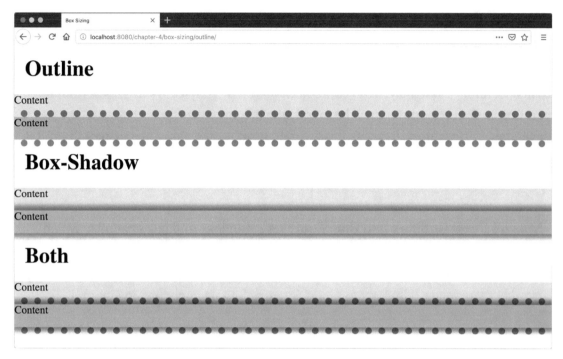

Figure 4-9. *Box-Shadow and Outline Do Not Occupy Space in the Layout*

Listing 4-5. HTML

```
<body>
  <h1>Outline</h1>
  <div class="container outline">
    <div>Content</div>
    <div>Content</div>
  </div>
  <h1>Box-Shadow</h1>
  <div class="container box-shadow">
    <div>Content</div>
    <div>Content</div>
  </div>
  <h1>Both</h1>
  <div class="container outline box-shadow">
    <div>Content</div>
    <div>Content</div>
  </div>
</body>
```

Listing 4-6. CSS

```css
.container div {
  background: rgba(0, 0, 0, .16); /* light grey */
  height: 50px;
}

.container div:last-of-type {
  background: rgba(0, 0, 0, .32); /* dark grey */
}

.container.outline div:last-of-type {
  outline: dotted 15px rgba(0, 0, 0, .5);
}

.container.box-shadow div:last-of-type {
  box-shadow: 0px 0px 10px 10px rgba(0, 0, 0, .5)
}
```

When both outline and box-shadow are set, they will overlap each other.

Border-Box

As described earlier, box-sizing: content-box has some disadvantages when mixins absolute units and percentage-based units. Content-box can also add extra complexity when setting content as a percentage of total width or height when the content has padding.

This is when border-box comes in. Assigning box-sizing: border-box changes how an element's width and height is calculated. Instead of encompassing just the content, it takes in the content, padding, and border. When padding or border is added, the width and height of the content itself is therefore decreased. See Figure 4-10.

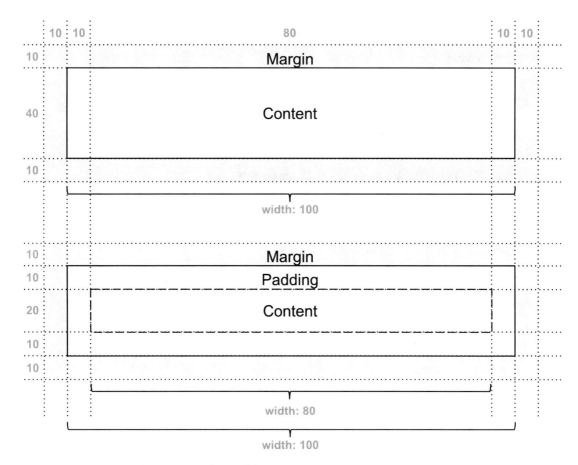

Figure 4-10. *Border-Box with Padding*

So if we take the first example of the two floated columns, we will see that the two columns retain a width of 50%. The margin still behaves the same way as with content-box. Listings 4-7 and 4-8 and Figure 4-11 show the same example as in Figure 4-4 using `box-sizing: border-box` instead of the default `box-sizing: content-box`.

Listing 4-7. HTML

```
<body>
  <h1>No Padding or Margin</h1>
  <div class="container">
    <div>
        <p>Content</p>
    </div>
```

```
    <div>
      <p>Content</p>
    </div>
  </div>

  <h1>With Padding</h1>
  <div class="container has-padding">
    <div>
      <p>Content</p>
    </div>
    <div>
      <p>Content</p>
    </div>
  </div>

  <h1>With Margin</h1>
  <div class="container has-margin">
    <div>
      <p>Content</p>
    </div>
    <div>
      <p>Content</p>
    </div>
  </div>
</body>
```

Listing 4-8. CSS

```
.container { overflow:auto; }
.container > div {
  width: 50%;
  box-sizing: border-box;
  float: left;
}
.container p {
  background: rgba(0, 0, 0, .16); /* light grey */
  text-align: center;
```

```
  margin: 0;
}
.container > div:last-of-type p { /* second rectangle */
  background: rgba(0, 0, 0, .32); /* dark grey */
}
.has-padding > div {
  border: dashed 1px rgba(0, 0, 0, .5);
  padding: 10px;
}
.has-margin > div {
  border: dashed 1px rgba(0, 0, 0, .5);
  margin: 10px;
}
```

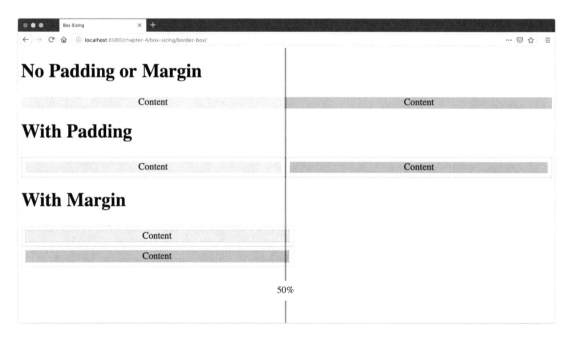

Figure 4-11. *Element Using Border-Box*

Box-sizing is not inherited. It will need to be applied to all elements for which it needs to be changed.

Display

Margin and padding allow for manipulating the display of the element; the display property manipulates how elements are displayed in relationship to one another by specifying the type of rendering the box uses for the element.

The display property has been at the cornerstone of layouts on the Web since the inception of CSS. Table 4-1 shows when each display value was added to the specification.

Table 4-1. *Display Property Values by CSS Version*[3]

Level 1	Level 2 (Revision 1)	Level 3
1996	2011	2018
block	inline-block	Contents
inline	table	flow-root
list-item	inline-table	run-in
none	table-row-group	inline list-item
	table-header-group	flex *
	table-footer-group	inline-flex *
	table-row table-column-group	grid *
	table-column	inline-grid *
	table-cell	ruby**
	table-caption	
	inherit	

*Candidate recommendation

**Working draft

Inline

Considered flow content, inline elements are placed inline with the text when in a flow layout. By default, the following elements are inline:

---

[3]Display. (August 4, 2019). Retrieved from `https://developer.mozilla.org/en-US/docs/Web/CSS/display`

`<a>`, `<abbr>`, `<acronym>`, `<audio>` (if it has visible controls), `<b>`, `<bdi>`, `<bdo>`, `<big>`, `<br>`, `<button>`, `<canvas>`, `<cite>`, `<code>`, `<command>`∗∗, `<data>`, `<datalist>`, `<del>`, `<dfn>`, `<em>`, `<embed>`, `<i>`, `<iframe>`, `<img>`, `<input>`, `<ins>`, `<kbd>`, `<keygen>`∗, `<label>`, `<map>`, `<mark>`, `<meter>`, `<noscript>`, `<object>`, `<output>`, `<picture>`, `<progress>`, `<q>`, `<ruby>`, `<s>`, `<samp>`, `<script>`, `<select>`, `<slot>`, `<small>`, `<span>`, `<strong>`, `<sub>`, `<sup>`, `<svg>`, `<template>`, `<textarea>`, `<time>`, `<u>`, `<tt>`, `<var>`, `<video>`, `<wbr>`[4]

*Deprecated
**Obsolete

When the content is displayed inline, by default elements go from left to right and set themselves side to side, width permitting. By default, elements, regardless of padding, and margin, will align themselves to the text baseline. If the width does not permit, the content will wrap below, as demonstrated in Figures 4-12 and 4-13 and Listings 4-9 and 4-10.

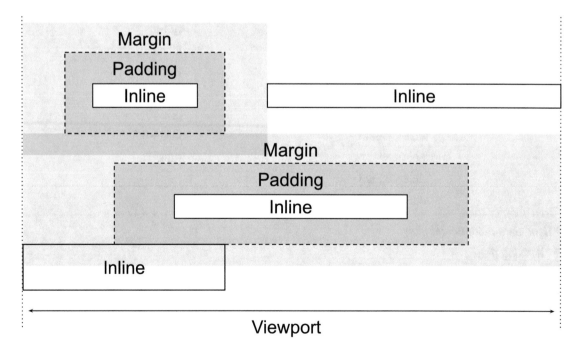

Figure 4-12. *Inline Elements*

---

[4]Inline elements. (August 4, 2019). Retrieved from https://developer.mozilla.org/en-US/docs/Web/HTML/Inline_elements

Listing 4-9. HTML

```
<body>
    I am some text.
    <span>I am a span.</span>
    More text goes here.
    <code>I am code.</code>
    And some more text.
    <a href="">I am an anchor tag.</a>
</body>
```

Listing 4-10. CSS

```
body {
  font-size: 24px;
  padding: 36px;
  margin: 0;
}

a {
  padding: 10px;
  outline: dotted 2px grey;
}

code {
  margin: 10px;
  outline: dotted 2px grey;
  outline-offset: 8px;
}
```

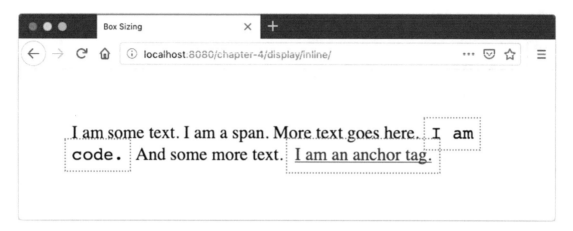

Figure 4-13. *Element Using border-box*

Block Elements

Also considered flow content, block elements stack atop one another unless they are affected by another property such as float.

The following elements are block-level elements by default:[5]

`<address>`, `<article>`, `<aside>`, `<blockquote>`, `<details>`, `<dialog>`, `<dd>`, `<div>`, `<dl>`, `<dt>`, `<fieldset>`, `<figcaption>`, `<figure>`, `<footer>`, `<form>`, `<h1>`, `<h2>`, `<h3>`, `<h4>`, `<h5>`, `<h6>`, `<header>`, `<hgroup>`, `<hr>`, `<li>`, `<main>`, `<nav>`, `<ol>`, `<p>`, `<pre>`, `<section>`, `<table>`, `<ul>`

Figures 4-14 and 4-15 show the default behavior for block-level elements.

---

[5]Block-level elements. (August 4, 2019). Retrieved from `https://developer.mozilla.org/en-US/docs/Web/HTML/Block-level_elements`

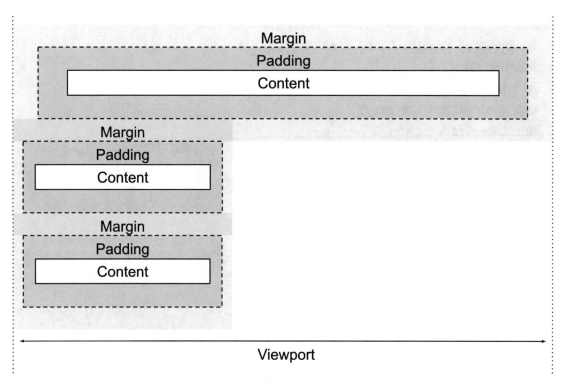

Figure 4-14. *Default Block-Level Behavior Diagram*

By default, block-level elements will take the full width of the viewport. If a width is applied, even if there is still enough room inline of the element, the block element will still place itself below the previous. See Listings 4-11 and 4-12.

Listing 4-11. HTML

```
<body>
  <div>Content</div>
  <div>Content</div>
  <div>Content</div>
</body>
```

Listing 4-12. CSS

```
html, body {
  font-size: 24px;
  padding: 36px;
  margin: 0;
}
```

91

```
div {
  background: rgba(0, 0, 0, .16);
  height: 50px;
  margin: 20px;
  outline: dotted 1px gray;
  outline-offset: 19px;
  text-align: center;
}

div:first-of-type {
  padding: 20px;
}

div:nth-of-type(2),
div:last-of-type {
  width: 200px;
}
```

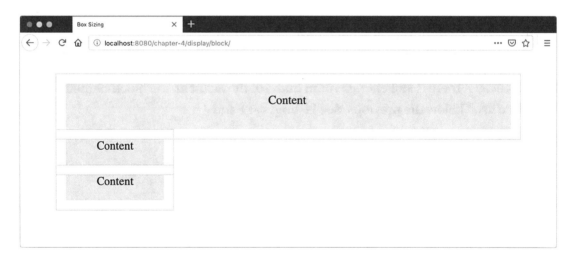

Figure 4-15. *Default Block-Level Behavior*

If an inline element is placed after a block element, the inline element will still be placed after the block element as seen in Listings 4-13, 4-14, and Figure 4-16.

Listing 4-13. HTML

```
<body>
  <div>Block Content</div>
  <span>Inline Content</span>
</body>
```

Listing 4-14. CSS

```
html, body {
  font-size: 24px;
  padding: 36px;
  margin: 0;
}

div {
  background: rgba(0, 0, 0, .16);
  height: 50px;
  width: 200px;
}
```

Figure 4-16. *Block and Inline*

Inline-Block

Inline-block utilizes concepts from both block and inline. It will behave like a block element but flow with the surrounding content as if it were inline. A common use case for inline-block is horizontal navigation; see Listings 4-15 and 4-16 and Figure 4-17.

Listing 4-15. Inline-Block HTML

```
<body>
  <nav>
    <ul>
      <li><a href="">Home</a></li>
      <li><a href="">About</a></li>
      <li><a href="">Contact</a></li>
    </ul>
  </nav>
</body>
```

Listing 4-16. Inline-Block CSS

```
html, body {
  font-size: 24px;
  padding: 36px;
  margin: 0;
}

ul {
  margin: 0;
  padding-left: 0;
  background: lightgray;
}
li {
  list-style-type: none;
  display: inline-block;
  margin: 2rem;
}
```

```
a {
  padding: 1rem 2rem;
  background: white;
  border-radius: 2rem;
}
```

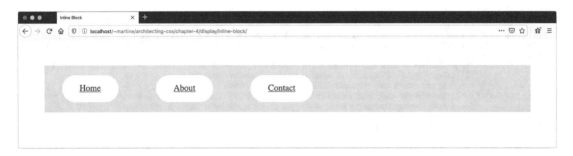

Figure 4-17. *Inline-Block*

The default behaviors of inline, block, and inline-block elements are not enough to create the layouts often desired. Before such options as grid and flex were introduced in 2018 or float, introduced until 1996,[6] we relied on tables even when the data was not tabular. For a long time, this was the only option in creating some more complex layouts, as even if the CSS specification described better methods, browsers did not necessarily support them. Today, this is no longer the case, and the use of tables for display purposes is now thoroughly frowned upon as it prevents assistive technologies from properly conveying the content being displayed to the users. Some exceptions, such as e-mail templates, still exist. Similarly to why historically they had been used for display purposes in web sites, most e-mail clients have little to no support for CSS layout properties, but the accessibility concerns remain and therefore tables for layout should be avoided whenever possible. For general web use, however, using tables for layouts is considered bad form and inaccessible. We are going to cover three commonly used patterns for laying out content: float, flexbox, and grid.

---

[6]Cascading Style Sheets, level 1. (December 17, 1996). Retrieved from www.w3.org/TR/CSS1/#float

Float

Unlike flex and grid, float is not part of the display property, but a property in and of itself.

A great use case for float is when a figure is included within text, allowing text to flow around the figure such as in Figure 4-18.

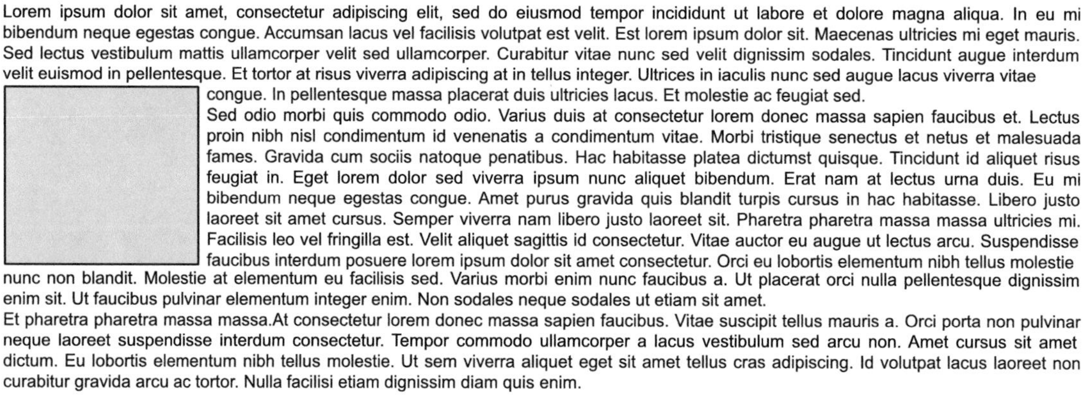

Lorem ipsum dolor sit amet, consectetur adipiscing elit, sed do eiusmod tempor incididunt ut labore et dolore magna aliqua. In eu mi bibendum neque egestas congue. Accumsan lacus vel facilisis volutpat est velit. Est lorem ipsum dolor sit. Maecenas ultricies mi eget mauris. Sed lectus vestibulum mattis ullamcorper velit sed ullamcorper. Curabitur vitae nunc sed velit dignissim sodales. Tincidunt augue interdum velit euismod in pellentesque. Et tortor at risus viverra adipiscing at in tellus integer. Ultrices in iaculis nunc sed augue lacus viverra vitae congue. In pellentesque massa placerat duis ultricies lacus. Et molestie ac feugiat sed.
Sed odio morbi quis commodo odio. Varius duis at consectetur lorem donec massa sapien faucibus et. Lectus proin nibh nisl condimentum id venenatis a condimentum vitae. Morbi tristique senectus et netus et malesuada fames. Gravida cum sociis natoque penatibus. Hac habitasse platea dictumst quisque. Tincidunt id aliquet risus feugiat in. Eget lorem dolor sed viverra ipsum nunc aliquet bibendum. Erat nam at lectus urna duis. Eu mi bibendum neque egestas congue. Amet purus gravida quis blandit turpis cursus in hac habitasse. Libero justo laoreet sit amet cursus. Semper viverra nam libero justo laoreet sit. Pharetra pharetra massa massa ultricies mi. Facilisis leo vel fringilla est. Velit aliquet sagittis id consectetur. Vitae auctor eu augue ut lectus arcu. Suspendisse faucibus interdum posuere lorem ipsum dolor sit amet consectetur. Orci eu lobortis elementum nibh tellus molestie nunc non blandit. Molestie at elementum eu facilisis sed. Varius morbi enim nunc faucibus a. Ut placerat orci nulla pellentesque dignissim enim sit. Ut faucibus pulvinar elementum integer enim. Non sodales neque sodales ut etiam sit amet.
Et pharetra pharetra massa massa.At consectetur lorem donec massa sapien faucibus. Vitae suscipit tellus mauris a. Orci porta non pulvinar neque laoreet suspendisse interdum consectetur. Tempor commodo ullamcorper a lacus vestibulum sed arcu non. Amet cursus sit amet dictum. Eu lobortis elementum nibh tellus molestie. Ut sem viverra aliquet eget sit amet tellus cras adipiscing. Id volutpat lacus laoreet non curabitur gravida arcu ac tortor. Nulla facilisi etiam dignissim diam quis enim.

Figure 4-18. *Floated Image*

Creating layouts using float, however, was much more difficult. Let's look at an example that uses the following HTML (Listing 4-17).

Listing 4-17. Example HTML

```
<body>
  <h1>Flexbox</h1>
  <nav>
    <ul>
      <li>Nav Element</li>
      <li>Nav Element</li>
      <li>Nav Element</li>
    </ul>
  </nav>
```

```
<div class="container">
  <section>
    <div><span>1</span></div>
    <div><span>2</span></div>
    <div><span>3</span></div>
  </section>
  <main>
    <h2>Main Content</h2>
    <p>Lorem ipsum dolor sit amet, consectetur... </p>
    <img src="./image.png" alt="">
    <p>Varius morbi enim nunc faucibus a. Ut placerat... </p>
    <p>Eget duis at tellus at urna condimentum mattis... </p>
  </main>
  <aside>
    <h2>Aside</h2>
    <p>Placerat duis ultricies lacus sed turpis tincidunt id aliquet... </p>
  </aside>
</div>
</body>
```

And we are going to try to achieve the layout in Figure 4-19.

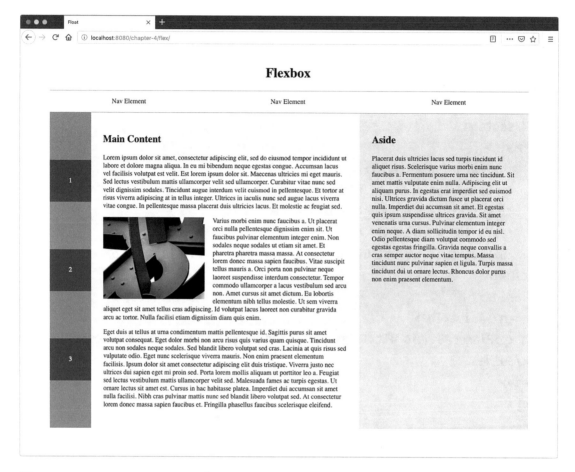

Figure 4-19. *Layout Example*

Starting with the navigation, we already see a problem in Figure 4-20 (Listings 4-18 and 4-19).

Listing 4-18. Float: CSS

```
html, body {
  padding: 36px;
  margin: 0;
}

h1 {
  text-align: center;
}
```

```
nav {
  border-top: solid 1px gray;
  border-bottom: solid 1px gray;
}
nav ul { padding: 0; }
nav li {
  list-style-type: none;
  width: 33%;
  float: left;
}
```

Once the list items are floated, the border rises up over them, and our numbers from the left-hand column come set themselves to the left of it (Figure 4-20).

Figure 4-20. *Floated Navigation*

In order for the numbers to behave, the float must be cleared. We can use display: flow-root on the list in order to clear the float. This is a fairly new property. Historically a class of "clearfix" or "group" (see Listing 4-19) would have been added to the list.

Listing 4-19. Clearfix

```
.clearfix::after {
  content: "";
  clear: both;
  display: table;
}
```

Continuing down the page, we can get close to the target layout (Figure 4-19) with floats (see Listing 4-20 and Figure 4-21); however, the column just doesn't line up at the bottom of the screen. Centering the numbers in the left column to look evenly distributed when the window is resized and the content reflows doesn't work either. Furthermore, since padding is used to center the numbers, if content was edited for a full sentence instead of a number, the padding would have to be recalculated or the text would no longer be centered.

Listing 4-20. CSS for Figure 4-21

```
html, body {
  padding: 36px;
  margin: 0;
}

h1 {
  text-align: center;
}
nav {
  border-top: solid 1px gray;
  border-bottom: solid 1px gray;
  display: flow-root;
}
nav ul {
  padding: 0;
  margin: 0;
}
nav li {
  box-sizing: border-box;
  list-style-type: none;
```

```
    float: left;
    padding: 1rem;
    text-align: center;
    width: 33.33%;
}

section {
    float: left;
    background: rgba(0, 0, 0, .16);
}
section div {
    box-sizing: border-box;
    color: white;
    background: rgba(0, 0, 0, .50);
    height: 100px;
    width: 100px;
    text-align: center;
    padding: 37px;
    margin-top: 5rem;
    margin-bottom: 5rem;
}

main {
    background: rgba(0, 0, 0, .05);
    box-sizing: border-box;
    padding: 30px;
    float: left;
    width: calc(100vw - 244px - 30%)
}

aside {
    box-sizing: border-box;
    background: rgba(0, 0, 0, .16);
    width: 30%;
    padding: 30px;
    float: right;
}
```

```
img {
  width: 100%;
  max-width: 250px;
  float: left;
  padding-right: 20px;
}
```

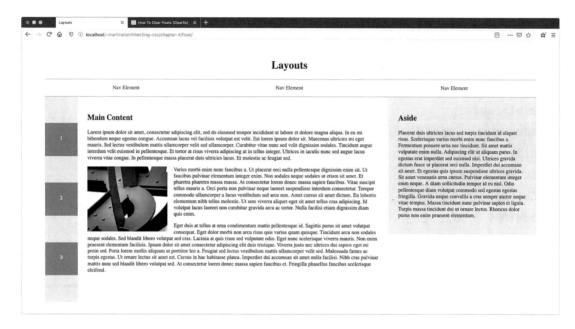

Figure 4-21. *Attempt a Layout Using Floats*

Getting the text around the image worked really well, as it is what float was designed to do. The rest of the layout had some issues, however. The padding and combination of a set height and width would more than likely make longer content expand out of its container in the far-left bar. Also of concern, 100% is not easily divisible by 3, so depending on how the browser decides to calculate the width of each nav element, content could be pushed around in ways it was not supposed to. Lastly the background on the columns just doesn't line up.

For all of these reasons, this would be a bug-prone and hard-to-maintain layout. To achieve this layout, and have the UI be fluid, the use of tables, the CSS `display: table` property, and/or JavaScript would have been required before flexbox and grid were introduced.

Flexbox

Historically, two types of layouts that were incredibly difficult, both found in the earlier example, included:

- Multiple columns where the background color is to align no matter the content within them

- Centering content vertically

Today we have flexbox. Solving those two problems is where flex really shines. Flexbox also allows for dynamically determining the width of the column based on the amount of content. Using display: flex is particularly useful when creating a layout that necessitates control over the spacing of elements across a container.

Let's try to create our layout again, using flexbox this time (Listing 4-21).

Listing 4-21. Flexbox CSS

```
h1 { text-align: center; }

nav {
  border-top: solid 1px gray;
  border-bottom: solid 1px gray;
}

ul {
  display: flex;
  padding-left: 0;
  justify-content: space-around;
}

.container { display: flex; }

aside {
  background: rgba(0, 0, 0, .16);
  flex-basis: 30%;
  flex-shrink: 0;
  padding: 30px;
}
```

```
section {
  background: rgba(0, 0, 0, .5);
  align-items: center;
  display: flex;
  flex-direction: column;
  justify-content: space-evenly;
}

section div {
  color: white;
  background: rgba(0, 0, 0, .50);
  align-items: center;
  display: flex;
  height: 100px;
  justify-content: center;
  width: 100px;
}

main {
  background: rgba(0, 0, 0, .05);
  padding: 30px;
}

li { list-style-type: none; }
img {
  width: 100%;
  max-width: 250px;
  float: left;
  padding-right: 20px;
}
```

Dissecting the preceding layout, we apply flex to three areas of the layout, the three content columns, the navigation, and the far-left column itself. For both the far-left column and in the navigation, flex is used in order to distribute the content across their container vertically and horizontally, respectively.

Flex-Direction

Flexbox is applied on two axes: main and cross. The main axis defines the direction of the layout. The property flex-direction is used on the container and includes four options: row, row-reverse, column, and column-reverse, where row is the default. This will determine the order in which elements will be displayed and the direction of the layout (see Figure 4-22).

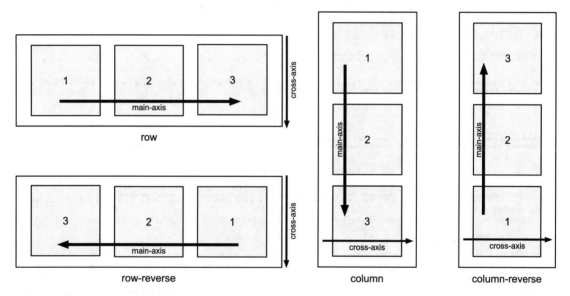

Figure 4-22. *Flexbox Main Axis*

Flexbox will by default try to fit all of the content onto one line but can be made to let the content wrap by using the flex-wrap property. The flex-wrap property can take any of the following values (Figure 4-23):

- **nowrap** – This is the default. All items will be placed on one line following the main axis and cause overflow if necessary.

- **wrap** – Items will wrap from top to bottom.

- **wrap-reverse** – Items will wrap from bottom to top.

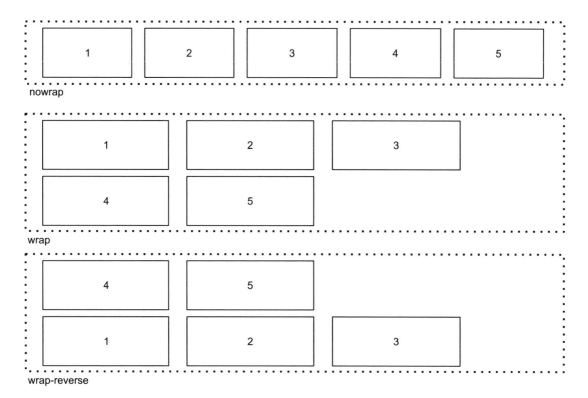

Figure 4-23. *Wrap*

By adding to row, column, or wrap, we can alter the sequence in which elements are displayed. If we want to move a specific element in the sequence individually, we can use order. The property takes an integer, by default 0. If an element is assigned a 1, and all others are set to the default 0, it will appear at the end. If assigned a -1, the element will appear at the beginning. The order is therefore based on the sequence provided and then weighted based on values assigned to each element using the order property.

Justify-Content

To determine the position of each element across the main axis, we use justify-content on the container. Possible values are as follows:

flex-start – Elements are placed at the beginning of the container. Flex-start is the default value.

First	Second	Third	

flex-end –Elements are placed at the end of the container.

	First	Second	Third

center – Elements are placed at the center of the container.

	First	Second	Third	

space-between – Elements are spaced evenly across the container with no space between the edges of the container and the first and last items.

First		Second		Third

space-around – Elements are spaced evenly across the container with half as much space between the edge of the container and the first and last items as between the other items.

	First		Second		Third	

space-evenly – Elements are spaced evenly across the container with the same amount of space between the edges and the first and last elements and between the elements.

	First		Second		Third	

Inline-Block   Flex-start, middle, and flex-end have some advantages over inline-block. For many use cases, the use of `display: inline-block` in conjunction with `text-align` can achieve the same result; however, inline-block has some intricacies regarding spacing. Even when margins are set to 0, a small gap will appear between elements. A layout where the sum of the elements equals 100% of the width of the container therefore becomes challenging to create. Let's look at the code and its output (Listings 4-22 and 4-23 and Figure 4-24).

Example 1

Listing 4-22. Inline-Block HTML

```
<body>
  <h1>Example 1</h1>
  <nav>
    <ul>
      <li>inline-block element</li>
      <li>inline-block element</li>
      <li>inline-block element</li>
    </ul>
  </nav>
</body>
```

Listing 4-23. Inline-Block CSS

```
html, body {
  padding: 12px 36px;
  margin: 0;
  font-size: 32px;
}

ul {
  padding-left: 0;
}
```

```
li {
  display: inline-block;
  padding: 10px 20px;
  background: grey;
  color: white;
}
```

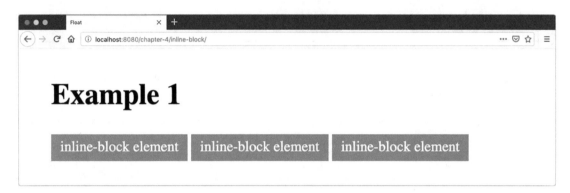

Figure 4-24. *Inline-Block Gap*

Notice the gap between the inline-block elements. There is no margin on the list element. Flexed items do not suffer from this unintended behavior.

Align-Items and Align-Self

The cross-axis is perpendicular to the main axis. Looking back at our original flexbox example (Figure 4-24), we have three columns of content, the left number section, the middle content section, and the right aside. For each of them to have the same length, denoted by their respective background colors aligning at the bottom, we can use the `align-content` property. The values are as follows:

   stretch – Elements will expand to the available height of the container (width if flex-direction is column).

	First		Second		Third	

For the purposes of columns, this behavior allows flexed elements to grow in size, similarly to a table row, so that all the elements included will have the same height as the latest in the array.

flex-start or start – Elements will align to the top of the container, similarly to `vertical-align: top`.

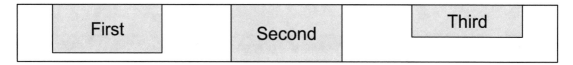

flex-end or end – Elements will align to the bottom of the container, similarly to `vertical-align: bottom`.

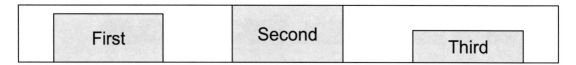

center – Elements will align to the middle of the container, similarly to `vertical-align: middle`.

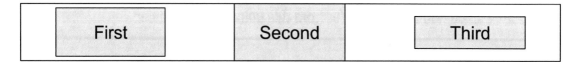

baseline – Elements will align to the text baseline, similarly to `vertical-align: baseline`.

The preceding properties are set on the container and will apply to all elements within. To manipulate a single element and make it behave differently from the others, we can use `align-self`. Its values are the same as those available for `align-items`, listed earlier.

Flex-Basis, Flex-Grow, and Flex-Shrink

Flex-basis allows for setting a base width elements should start at. Their content will determine whether they need to grow or shrink to fit the space available in the container.

To ensure that content fills 100% of the available space in the container, a **flex-grow** property can be applied. By default set to 0, it specifies the growth factor of the flexed item. This value is ratio based. If all siblings of the container have the same value, then they will all grow by the same amount so that the sum of the elements equals 100% of the available width (or height if flex-direction is set to column). Otherwise it will be distributed according to the ratio defined on each flexed element.

Flex-shrink works similarly to flex-grow but for shrinking content to prevent overflow. By default set to 1, it can be set to 0 and used in conjunction with flex-basis to ensure a flexed element has a fixed width (or height if flex-direction is set to column).

Because of its ability to dynamically deal with the space provided, display-flex makes generating fluid designs and aligning content easier than ever before, without resorting to the use of tables for display purposes but it is very one directional. Grid, however, brings in the second dimension.

Grid

Also fairly recently introduced is grid. Where grid shines is that it gives the developer the ability to name sections making the code easy to read and maintain. Unlike flexbox which only deals with one direction at a time, grid allows for rows and columns to be defined. These sections can be names such as in Listing 4-24, or based on the row and column number such as in Listing 4-26.

Listing 4-24. Grid CSS

```
.container {
 display: grid;
 grid-template-columns: 1fr 1fr 1fr 300px;
 grid-template-rows: 46px auto 36px;
 grid-template-areas:
    "header header header header"
    "main main . sidebar"
    "footer footer footer sidebar";
}
```

Grid-template-columns defines four columns. The first three of equal width and the last of 300px. The "fr" unit used here represents a fraction of leftover space as a ratio.[7] The last column will be given a width of 300 pixels; the other three will receive equal amounts of leftover space as their width.

Grid-template-rows defines three rows, the first with height and last with height of 46 and 36 pixels, respectively. The middle row, set to auto, will adjust its height to accommodate its content.

Grid-template-areas defines, on the 4 by 3 grid just created, named areas by row as seen in Figure 4-25.

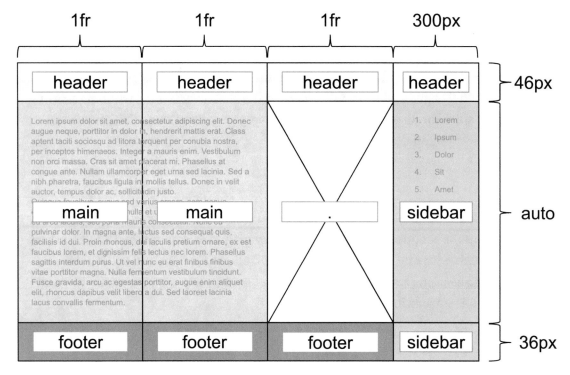

Figure 4-25. *Grid Template Areas*

So looking at a full implementation, the code will look and output looks as follows (Listings 4-25 and 4-26). Figure 4-26 displays the output.

---

[7]CSS Grid Layout MOdule Level 1: 7.2.3. Flexible Lengths: the "fr" unit. (August 5, 2019).
Retrieved from www.w3.org/TR/css3-grid-layout/#fr-unit

Listing 4-25. Grid HTML

```
<body>
  <div class="container">
    <header>
      <h2>Header</h2>
    </header>
    <main>
      <h2>Main</h2>
      <p>Lorem ipsum dolor sit amet, consectetur… </p>
      <p>Quisque faucibus, augue sed varius ornare… </p>
    </main>
    <aside class="sidebar">
      <h2>Sidebar</h2>
      <ol>
        <li>Lorem</li>
        <li>Ipsum</li>
        <li>Dolor</li>
        <li>Sit</li>
        <li>Amet</li>
      </ol>
    </aside>
    <footer>
      <h2>Footer</h2>
    </footer>
  </div>
</body>
```

Listing 4-26. Grid CSS

```
html, body {
  padding: 36px;
  margin: 0;
}
```

```css
header {
  grid-area: header;
  background: rgba(0, 0, 0, .1);
  text-align: center;
  padding: 5px;
}
main {
  grid-area: main;
  background: rgba(0, 0, 0, .2);
  padding: 10px;
}
.sidebar {
  grid-area: sidebar;
  padding: 10px;
  background: rgba(0, 0, 0, .3);
}
footer {
  grid-area: footer;
  background: rgba(0, 0, 0, .5);
  text-align: center;
  color: white;
}
.container {
 display: grid;
 grid-template-columns: 1fr 1fr 1fr 1fr;
 grid-template-rows: 46px auto 36px;
 grid-template-areas:
    "header header header header"
    "main main . sidebar"
    "footer footer footer sidebar";
}

header, footer {
  display: flex;
  align-items: center;
  justify-content: center;
```

```
}
header h2, footer h2 {
  margin: 0;
}
```

Note the " . " on the second row of the grid-template-areas for the container class; this allows for the three-column/second row grid section to remain empty.

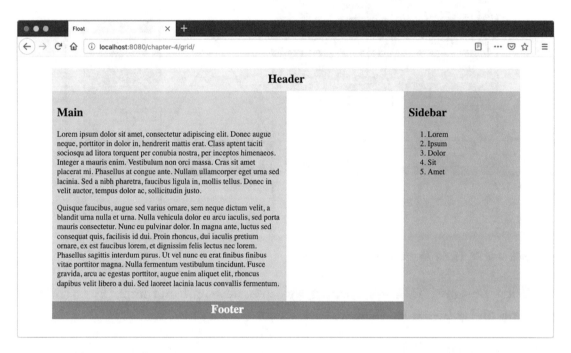

Figure 4-26. *Grid Output*

Each UI element is set to its named grid-area. The advantage is the naming can follow the purpose of the container being positioned, making the code easy to read and then maintain. Furthermore, when repositioning elements for responsiveness, the only property that needs to be updated is the grid-template-areas.

Grid also allows for defining areas using column and row numbers. Numbering starts at 1 on the far left for columns and 1 on the very top for rows as depicted in Figure 4-27.

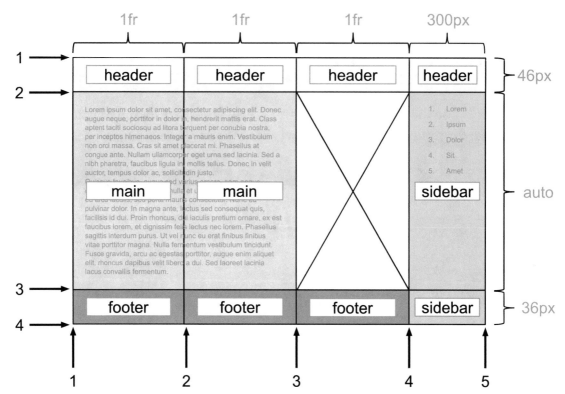

Figure 4-27. *Grid Rows and Columns*

Using the same HTML and as earlier, we can achieve the same output by assigning grid-row and grid-column values to each section (Listing 4-27).

Listing 4-27. Grid CSS

```
html, body {
  padding: 36px;
  margin: 0;
}

header {
  grid-area: header;
  background: rgba(0, 0, 0, .1);
  text-align: center;
  padding: 5px;
  grid-row: 1;
  grid-column: 1 / 5;
}
```

```
main {
  grid-area: main;
  background: rgba(0, 0, 0, .2);
  padding: 10px;
  grid-row: 2;
  grid-column: 1;
}
.sidebar {
  grid-area: sidebar;
  padding: 10px;
  background: rgba(0, 0, 0, .3);
  grid-row: 2 / 4;
  grid-column: 4;
}
footer {
  grid-area: footer;
  background: rgba(0, 0, 0, .5);
  text-align: center;
  color: white;
  grid-row: 3;
  grid-column: 1 / 4;
}
.container {
 display: grid;
 grid-template-columns: 1fr 1fr 1fr 1fr;
 grid-template-rows: 46px auto 36px;
}

header, footer {
  display: flex;
  align-items: center;
  justify-content: center;
}
header h2, footer h2 {
  margin: 0;
}
```

Grid-row and grid-column can be defined using a single integer (grid-row: 1) or two integers separated by a / (grid-row: 1/3). When only one integer is used, the section will start that the line specified and span one column or row such as for the main element in the example earlier. When two integers separated by a / are used, the section will start at the line specified by the first integer and end at the line specified by the second, as seen on the footer's grid-column value.

Similarly to flexbox or table, the placement of content within a section can be adjusted. The justify-items property can be used on the grid container to determine how content within sections or cells will align left to right. Its values are start, end, center, and stretch as illustrated in Figure 4-28. Stretch is the default value.

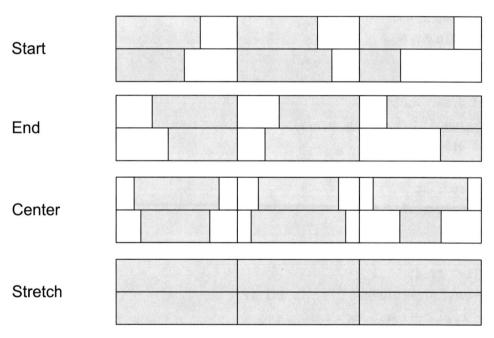

Figure 4-28. *Justify-Items Values*

The same values can be used to change the alignment of a specific cell using the justify-self property on the specific section.

To specify how content aligns vertically in a cell, we can assign the align-items property to the grid container. Its values are the same as earlier and it also defaults to stretch (Figure 4-29).

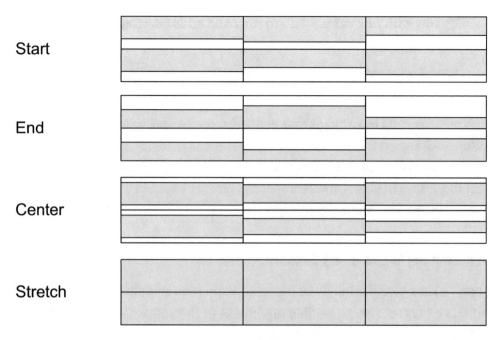

Figure 4-29. *Vertical Alignment Using Align-Items*

Similarly to `justify-self`, the same values can be used with the `align-self` property on an individual section to allow for a cell to behave differently than the default set on the container.

Just like flexbox, grid also has a justify-content and an align-items property. They have the same values and work in the same fashion as for flexbox. They position grid cells horizontally and vertically within the container. This can be very useful when the grid itself is smaller than the grid container.

To add space between the cells, grid-gap can be used. This will determine how much space is between each row and/or column. Individually, they can be set using grid-row-gap and grid-column-gap, respectively. For example, `grid-gap: 5px 2rem` would set a gap of 5 pixels between each row and a gap of 2 rems between each column.

Lastly, grid has an auto-placement algorithm. This will kick in when there are more items to place than what is defined by the CSS, or when an element has a grid-column or a grid-row value that is outside of the bounds defined in the container's templates. The behavior of the auto-placement is controlled using the grid-auto-flow property. Auto-flow can be optimized for filling

- **By row with row value** – Fills in rows and adds new rows as necessary

- **By column, using the column value** – Fills in columns and adds new columns as necessary

To have the grid fill in any gaps that may exist, dense may be added to both the row and column values, `grid-auto-flow: column dense`.

Grid is now much more widely supported across evergreen browsers but has some compatibility issues in older browsers such as Internet Explorer 11 which currently has an incomplete implementation of the specification.

⊛ Accessibility When Using Flexbox or Grid

Grid and flexbox give the ability to reposition and reorder content at will simply by changing just one or two properties regardless of the sequence in the HTML. This can become problematic for accessibility.

The Web Content Accessibility Guidelines states

> When the sequence in which content is presented affects its meaning, a correct reading sequence can be programmatically determined. (Level A) Criterion 1.3.2 Meaningful Sequence (Level A)[8]

When changing the order of elements using CSS, it is important to make sure the programmatic sequence still makes sense.

Responsive Design

At the core of responsive design implementation is the media query.

---

[8]Web Content Accessibility Guidelines (WCAG) 2.0, Meaningful Sequence. (August 7, 2019). Retrieved from `www.w3.org/TR/2008/REC-WCAG20-20081211/#content-structure-separation-sequence`

> **Media Query**   "Media Queries allow authors to test and query values or features of the user agent or display device, independent of the document being rendered. They are used in the CSS **@media** rule to conditionally apply styles to a document, and in various other contexts and languages, such as HTML and JavaScript."
>
> —Media Queries Level 4[9]

More specifically, using media queries allows you to conditionally change styles based on the viewport's properties. Often used in responsive design are media queries related to the viewport's width, the end goal being to tailor the layout for small mobile screens vs. large desktop monitors, and everything in between. To achieve this technique, breakpoints are chosen at different viewport width(s) where the styles will change. The CSS might look as in Listing 4-28.

Listing 4-28.   Media Query

```
@media (min-width: 500px) { ... }
```

where anything in between the brackets does not get applied unless the width of the viewport is greater than 500px. Width ranges can also be declared this way (Listing 4-29).

Listing 4-29.   Ranged Media Query

```
@media (500px <= width <= 700px) { ... }
```

where the styles are applied when the viewport widths are between 500 and 700 pixels.

It is easy to fall into the trap of thinking that the styles need to be rewritten for each of the breakpoints. Furthermore, when going from narrow to wide layouts, far fewer styles need to be overridden than going from wide to narrow. This is because on narrower layouts, items are more likely to be simply stacked than with wide layouts. For most use cases, the easiest way to set up responsiveness to decrease the amount of code being written is to start with the narrow layout and then add on as the screen gets wider. Let's look at the implementation of this sample design (Figure 4-30).

---

[9]Media Queries Level 4. (August 9, 2019). Retrieved from www.w3.org/TR/mediaqueries-4/

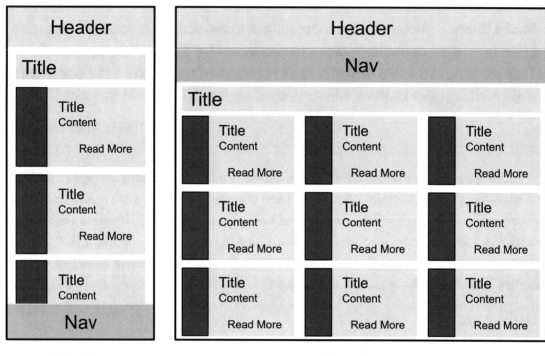

Figure 4-30. *Responsive Design*

To achieve this layout, the HTML in Listing 4-30 will be used.

Listing 4-30. Responsive Layout HTML

```
<body>
  <header>
    <h1>Responsive Design</h1>
  </header>
  <nav>
    <ul>
      <li><a href="">Link 1</a></li>
      <li><a href="">Link 2</a></li>
      <li><a href="">Link 3</a></li>
    </ul>
```

```
    </nav>
    <h2>My Items</h2>
    <main>
      <article>
        <h3>Article Title</h3>
        <p>Lorem ipsum dolor sit amet, consectetur elit...</p>
        <a href="">Read More</a>
      </article>
      ...
    </main>
</body>
```

The first thing we do is establish some base styles that will be applied regardless of screen size (Listing 4-31).

Listing 4-31. Base Styles

```
html, body {
  margin: 0;
  padding: 0;
}

body {
  box-sizing: border-box;
  font-family: 'Gill Sans', 'Gill Sans MT', ... sans-serif;
  height: 100vh;
  left: 0;
  margin: 0;
  position: absolute;
  top: 0;
  width: 100vw;
}

h1, h2, h3 {
  font-family: Impact, Haettenschweiler, ... sans-serif;
  margin: 0;
}
```

```css
header {
  background: rgba(0, 0, 0, .1);
  box-sizing: border-box;
  grid-area: header;
  text-align: center;
  padding: .75rem;
}

nav {
  background: #c6c6c6;
  grid-area: nav;
}
nav ul {
  margin: 0;
  padding: 0;
  display: flex;
  justify-content: space-evenly;
}
nav li { list-style-type: none; }
nav a {
  display: block;
  padding: 1rem;
}

h2 {
  background: #c6c6c6;
  grid-area: title;
  padding: .5rem 1rem;
}

main {
  padding: 1rem;
  grid-area: main;
  overflow: auto;
}
```

```
article {
  background: #e9e9e9;
  border-left: solid 2.5rem gray;
  padding: 1rem;
  margin-bottom: 1rem;
}
article a {
  display: block;
  text-align: right;
}
```

We can then add the layout-specific information for each breakpoint (Listings 4-32 and 4-33).

Listing 4-32. Mobile CSS

```
/* Mobile layout */
body {
  display: grid;
  grid-template-columns: 1fr;
  grid-template-rows: 4rem auto auto 3rem;
  grid-template-areas:
    "header"
    "title"
    "main"
    "nav";
  height: 100vh;
  overflow: hidden;
}
```

Listing 4-33. Desktop CSS

```
/* Desktop layout */
@media (min-width: 500px) {
  body {
    grid-template-columns: 1fr;
    grid-template-rows: auto auto auto;
```

```
   grid-template-areas:
     "header"
     "nav"
     "title"
     "main";
   height: auto;
   overflow: auto;
 }

 main { column-width: 250px ; }
 article { break-inside: avoid; }
 h2 { background: none; }
}
```

Notice that in Listing 4-33, it takes very little CSS to readjust the layout for desktop users. This is because base styles are already applied and do not have to be duplicated. We also see here the advantages of named areas for grid layout and the ease of organizing them for the correct layout.

Summary

Elements are subject to the box model, which dictates how its width, padding, margin, and border will behave. When put together, the elements form a layout. There are as many ways to approach a layout as there are layouts to be created, but each technique has its own strengths and weaknesses. We have looked at float, flexbox, and grid as well as media queries for responsive layouts.

In the next chapter, we will look at scenarios where CSS doesn't seem to work as expected, with a special focus on differences between browsers.

CHAPTER 5

Compatibility and Defaults

When writing CSS, it doesn't take very long for most developers to realize that the same code, when run in different browsers or even on the same browser but on a different device, just doesn't behave in the same way. This chapter covers browser differences and techniques to handle cross-browser compatibility.

Browser Support

When testing a layout, it is important to test the application in multiple browsers, because they do not all use the same layout and JavaScript engines, which lead to variation in how they interpret code. Table 5-1 lists some common browsers and their engines.

Table 5-1. *Browser Technologies*

Browser	Layout Engine	JavaScript Engine
Chrome	Blink, WebKit	V8
Firefox	Gecko, Quantum	SpiderMonkey
Internet Explorer	Trident	Chakra, JScript
Microsoft Edge	EdgeHTML, WebKit (on IOS), Blink (on Android) – switching to a Chromium platform[1]	Chakra
Opera	Blink (Chromium)	Chrome V8
Safari	WebKit	Nitro

---

[1]Warren, T. (8 April 2019). Retrieved on September 3, 2019, from www.theverge.com/2019/4/8/18300077/microsoft-edge-chromium-canary-development-release-download

127

© Martine Dowden and Michael Dowden 2020
M. Dowden and M. Dowden, *Architecting CSS*, https://doi.org/10.1007/978-1-4842-5750-0_5

The layout engine is responsible for how the page should look. It determines, based on the CSS, how the view should be laid out, painted, and animated. See Chapter 1 for rendering details. Furthermore, many are available as open source and are maintained by different groups and agencies, allowing for differences in the implementation and status of any given specification.

For example, the scroll-snap-type CSS property, part of the Scroll Type Module whose first public draft was published in March of 2015 and now is a candidate for recommendation, has[2] vastly different support and implementation across browsers. This leads to behavior differences. See Table 5-2 for browser-specific support details.

***Table 5-2.** Browser Support for Scroll Snap by Browser Version[3]*

Chrome	Firefox	Internet Explorer	Microsoft Edge	Opera	Safari
4 - 65	-	-	-	-	3.1 - 8
66 - 68	2 - 38	6 - 9	-	10 - 53	9 - 10.1
69 - 75	39 - 67	10	12 - 17	54 - 60	11 - 12
76	68	11	18	62	12.1
77 - 79	69 - 70		76		13 - TP

Not Supported	Partial, incomplete, or supports older specification	Supported

Looking over time, it is clear that using this property would yield different results across browsers. Furthermore, browsers include CSS defaults, and these also have slight differences.

---

[2]CSS Scroll Snap Module Level 1 Publication History. Retrieved September 1, 2019, from www.w3.org/standards/history/css-scroll-snap-1

[3]Can I use scroll-snap? Retrieved September 1, 2019, from https://caniuse.com/#search=scroll-snap

Browser Defaults

When writing HTML where no CSS is applied, certain tags have default styles such as the header tags (see Figure 5-1).

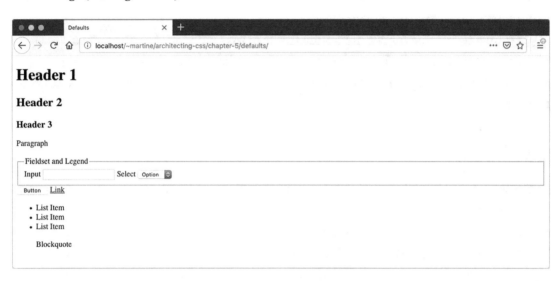

Figure 5-1. *Default Styles*

Browsers, however, don't use the same style sheets and therefore don't have the same default. Although mostly similar, there are some subtle differences. Textarea, for example, will behave differently in Safari vs. Firefox (see Figures 5-2 and 5-3).

Figure 5-2. *Firefox*

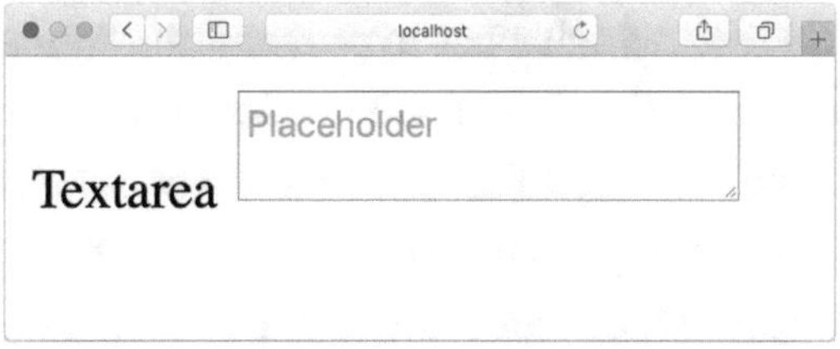

Figure 5-3. *Safari*

Notice the default typeface in the textarea; in Firefox it is a monospaced font vs. a sans-serif in Safari. The alignment also differs slightly. On Firefox, the textarea is aligned to the baseline of the text, while in Safari it hovers slightly above the baseline. These subtle differences can be infuriating when trying to get a design to look and behave the same across browsers and versions.

A robust technique for counteracting this is to manually set defaults so that all browsers are running off the same base styles. Although this does not address compatibility differences, it will address subtle unintended behavior differences such as the one outlined earlier.

CSS Reset

CSS reset is a file that takes all the defaults sets on elements by the browsers and "resets" them. The goal is to take element styles and bring them all to the same consistent baseline in order to reduce or eliminate inconsistencies that exist between browsers. There are many options out there, but a commonly used one is by Eric Meyer (see Table 5-3), one of the pioneers of CSS reset. Whichever one you use, there isn't a one size fits all, and it probably will need to be customized to your particular project.

Table 5-3. *CSS Reset*

Reference	Link
Project Site	https://meyerweb.com/eric/tools/css/reset/index.html
Style sheet	https://meyerweb.com/eric/tools/css/reset/reset.css

Normalize

Normalize is a project published by Nicolas Gallagher and Jonathan Neal in August of 2016. It focuses on fixing known differences between browsers. This approach is radically different to a CSS reset which aims to prevent differences by flattening the default styles. Normalize retains the defaults. By adding normalize as the first CSS to be loaded in a project, either by making it the first style sheet to be imported or by including it in the project's CSS as the first CSS to be applied, the variations are already dealt with and focus can shift to achieving the layout rather than fighting with subtle differences between browsers (for where to find normalize, see Table 5-4). Worth pointing out is that many CSS frameworks and libraries, such as Bootstrap, already include some form of normalization. It is worth double-checking that any UI library or framework being used doesn't already account for differences to prevent unnecessary bloat.

Table 5-4. *Normalize*

Reference	Link
Project Site	http://necolas.github.io/normalize.css/
GitHub Repository	https://github.com/necolas/normalize.css
NPM	www.npmjs.com/package/normalize.css
CDN	https://yarnpkg.com/en/package/normalize.css
Style sheet	https://necolas.github.io/normalize.css/latest/normalize.css

Although normalizing base styles addresses differences in CSS defaults, it does not address differences in implementation or support.

Note   Normalize and reset are not being endorsed in any way, and the quality and relevance of any package can be subject to rapid change. Please research any dependencies you intend to use.

Browser Compatibility

Cross-browser compatibility, making sure the UI looks the same across multiple browsers, ranks right up there among the hardest things to do in CSS. There are multiple ways to tackle this problem and they are often used in combination with one another.

Vendor Prefixes

When functionality for a browser is still experimental or is nonstandard, browsers used to make them available using vendor-specific prefixes. Although this may help in reaching similarity across user agents, using CSS that relies on vendor prefixes in production is not a good idea as the implementation is experimental and may not follow the specification. Because historically developers have been using these prefixes in production, browsers are increasingly moving to placing nonstandard and experimental features behind feature flags to end this practice; however, many are still actively in use (see Table 5-5).[4]

Table 5-5. *Vendor Prefixes*

Prefix	Browsers
-webkit-	WebKit-based browsers (Chrome, Safari, etc.)
-moz-	Firefox
-o-	Pre-WebKit versions of Opera
-ms-	Internet Explorer and Microsoft Edge

Internet Explorer 11 (IE), for example, has a nonstandard implementation of grid. Its implementation is based on the April 7, 2011, working draft rather than the candidate recommendation.[5] Therefore, vendor prefixes must be used in order for grid to work in IE. However, even with the use of prefixes, behavior still differs. In IE, explicitly positioning each element in the grid is necessary but not in other browsers where they will set themselves in the next available space. Furthermore, some aspects of the current specification, such as grid-gap, are simply missing. Listings 5-2 and 5-3 show the code to achieve the same layout in IE and Firefox when using grid. Both will use the same HTML (Listing 5-1). Their respective outputs are shown in Figures 5-4 and 5-6, while Figure 5-5 shows IE without vendor prefixes.

Listing 5-1. Grid HTML

```
<body>
  <div class="grid-container">
    <aside>My Aside</aside>
    <section>Section 1</section>
    <section>Section 2</section>
    <section>Section 3</section>
    <section>Section 4</section>
  </div>
</body>
```

---

[4]Vendor Prefix. Retrieved September 1, 2019, from https://developer.mozilla.org/en-US/ docs/Glossary/Vendor_Prefix

[5]Can I use grid? Retrieved September 1, 2019, from https://caniuse.com/#search=grid

Listing 5-2. Grid Without Vendor Prefixes

```
html, body {
  padding: 36px;
  margin: 0;
}

.grid-container {
  display: grid;
  grid-template-columns: 1fr 1fr 1fr;
  grid-template-rows: 5rem 5rem;
  grid-gap: 1rem;
}

aside {
  grid-row: 1/3;
  background: lightgray;
}

section {
  border: solid 1px gray;
}
```

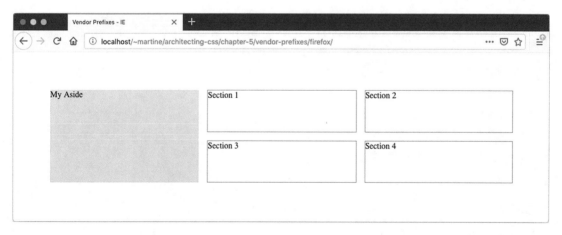

Figure 5-4. *Grid in Firefox*

When the same code found in Listing 5-2 is run in IE, no grid is rendered and the elements are simply stacked on top of each other (Figure 5-5).

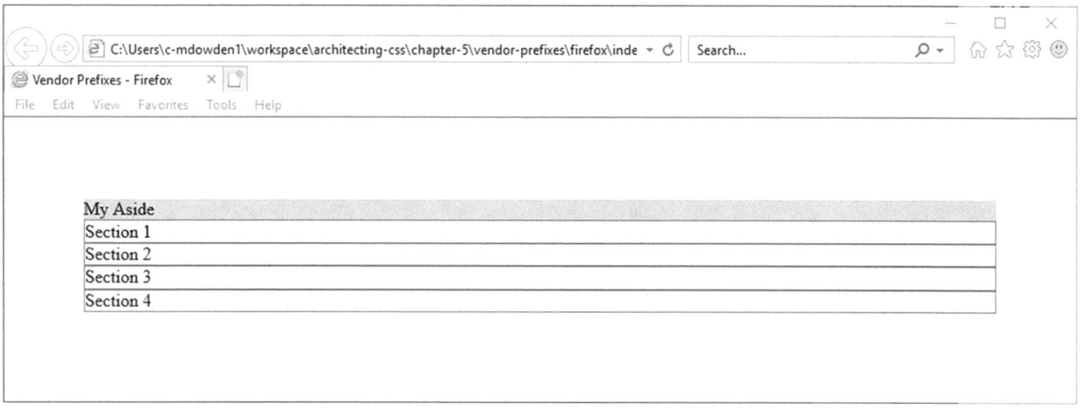

Figure 5-5. *Grid Without Vendor Prefixes in IE*

This is because grid, a value of display, does not exist. To access grid functionality in Internet Explorer, vendor prefixes need to be used.

Listing 5-3. Grid with Internet Explorer Vendor Prefixes

```
html, body {
  padding: 36px;
  margin: 0;
}

.grid-container {
  margin: -.5rem;
  display: -ms-grid;
  -ms-grid-columns: 1fr 1fr 1fr;
  -ms-grid-rows: 5rem 5rem;
}

aside {
  background: lightgray;
  -ms-grid-row-span: 2;
  margin: .5rem;
}
```

```
section {
  border: solid 1px gray;
  margin: .5rem;
}
section:nth-of-type(1) {
  -ms-grid-column: 2;
  -ms-grid-row: 1;
}
section:nth-of-type(2) {
  -ms-grid-column: 3;
  -ms-grid-row: 1;
}
section:nth-of-type(3) {
  -ms-grid-column: 2;
  -ms-grid-row: 2;
}
section:nth-of-type(4) {
  -ms-grid-column: 3;
  -ms-grid-row: 2;
}
```

With -ms vendor prefix and substituting grid-gap for margins, the same layout can be achieved (Figure 5-6).

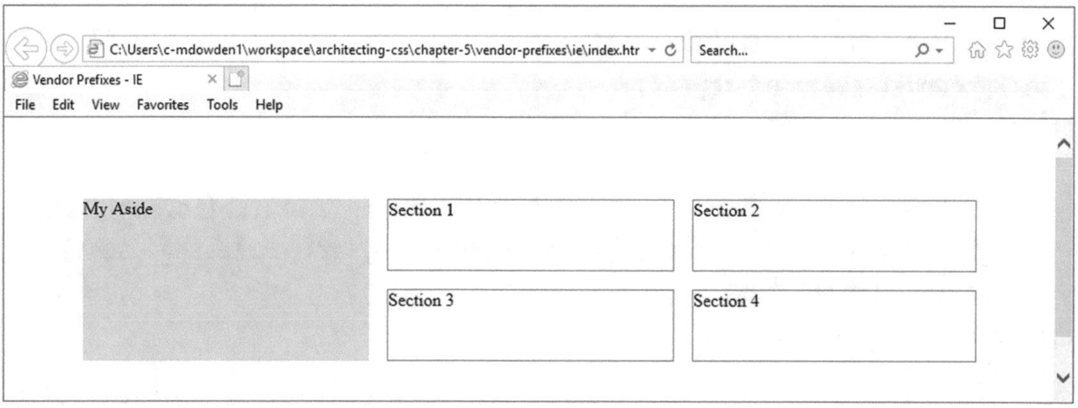

Figure 5-6. *Grid with Vendor Prefixes in IE*

Fallbacks

A better solution to vendor prefixes when a browser does not support a property is to create a fallback. When a browser encounters a property or value it does not support, it will ignore it, and therefore, the previously set value will be maintained. If the element does not have a previously set value or does not inherit a value, the default will be used.

For example, (at the time of this writing) cross-fade has an experimental version, behind a vendor prefix (-webkit) in Safari and is unsupported in Firefox. To start using it, a fallback can be created. Listings 5-4 and 5-5 show the use of cross-fade and its fallback (Figure 5-8 shows the desired output).

Listing 5-4. Cross-Fade Fallback HTML

```
<body>
  <div class="container"></div>
</body>
```

Listing 5-5. Cross-Fade Fallback CSS

```
html, body {
  box-sizing: border-box;
  padding: 36px;
  margin: 0;
}

.container {
  background-image: url(child.png);
  background-repeat: no-repeat;
  background-size: contain;
  background-position: bottom;
  background-image: -webkit-cross-fade(url(beach.png), url(child.png), 50%);
  background-image: cross-fade(url(beach.png) 50%, url(child.png) 50% );
  box-sizing: border-box;
  padding: 1rem;
  height: 30rem;
  max-width: 100%;
  width: 100%;
}
```

First, a background image is set, then it is overridden by the cross-fade using the vendor prefix, and finally, it is overridden again by the standard cross-fade. Browsers that don't support cross-fade or the vendor prefix version, such as Firefox (Figure 5-7), will display just the background image.

Figure 5-7. *Fallback to Background Image*

Browsers which do support a vendor prefix, such as Safari (Figure 5-8), will display the experimental versions.

Figure 5-8. *Cross-Fade*

Finally, browsers that support the final version will display the specification-defined cross-fade.

Supports At-Rule

The @supports at-rule allows for checking if a particular property and value pair is supported or not, allowing the user experience to be customized accordingly.
This feature is generally well supported apart from IE. The expression @supports(property:value {} returns true when the property is supported, while @supports not (property:value){} is true for when it is not. Styles within the selector are only applied if the selector returns true. These can be conjoined with either the and or or operators to create new expressions. Generally it is prefered to use @supports for progressive enhancement of newer features, while fallbacks can be used to provide backwards-compatibility with older browsers.

To see @supports in action, let's look at the backdrop filter, which works in Opera but not in Firefox. Listings 5-6 and 5-7 show the use of @supports to create conditional styling using support.

Listing 5-6. Cross-Fade Fallback HTML

```
<body>
  <div class="container">
    <p>Lorem ipsum dolor sit amet, consectetur adipiscing</p>
  </div>
</body>
```

Listing 5-7. Cross-Fade Fallback CSS

```
html, body {
  padding: 36px;
  margin: 0;
}

.container {
  background-image: url('art.png');
  padding: 1rem;
}
p {
  background-color: rgba(255, 255, 255, 0.6);
  backdrop-filter: blur(20px);
  margin: 5rem;
  padding: 1rem;
}

@supports not (backdrop-filter: blur(20px) ) {
  p {
    background-color:white;
  }
}
```

When backdrop-filter is supported, the paragraph background is blurred and at a 60% opacity (Figure 5-9). When it isn't, the paragraph background is set to white with full opacity to increase legibility that would have been gained from blur (Figure 5-10).

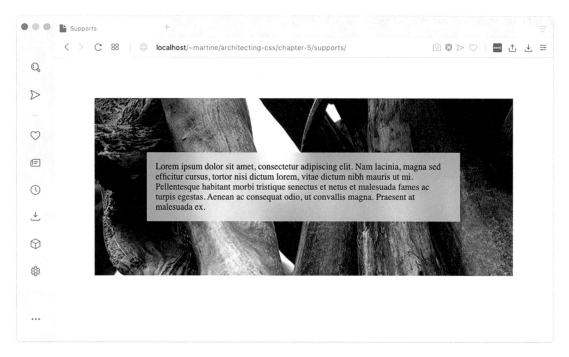

Figure 5-9. `backdrop-filter`

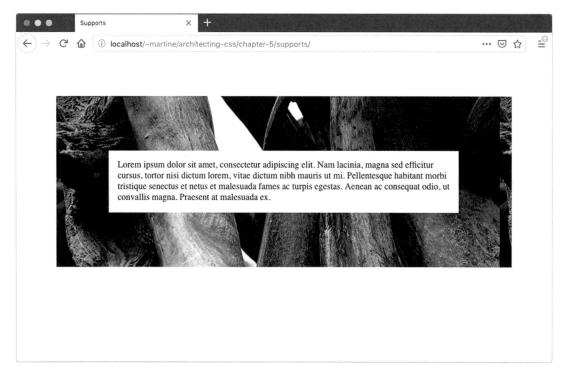

Figure 5-10. *Fallback*

Project Defaults

Resetting browser defaults helps with creating consistency across browsers. Creating application defaults can help create consistency across the application. This is especially important when working with component-based architectures. Separating out theme from layout will also help with consistency. Style can be set on the elements themselves and base classes to be reused throughout the application. If the theme is changed, these changes only need to be updated in one place. Furthermore, when creating new views, the only concern becomes layout as the theme is already taken care of. Listings 5-8 and 5-9 are a sample excerpt; Figure 5-11 shows the output.

Listing 5-8. Default Styles HTML

```
<body class="view">
  <h1>Theme</h1>
  <div class="container">
    <div class="card">
      <div class="header">Header</div>
      <div class="body">
        <p>Lorem ipsum dolor sit amet, ... </p>
      </div>
      <div class="actions">
        <button>My Button</button>
        <a>My Link</a>
      </div>
    </div>
    <div class="card"> ... </div>
    <div class="card"> ... </div>
  </div>
</body>
```

Listing 5-9. Default Styles CSS

```
body {
  --border: solid 1px rgba(0, 0, 0, .2);
  --dark: rgba(0, 0, 0, .87);
  --light: rgba(255, 255, 255, .87);
```

```
  --shadow: box-shadow: 5px 5px 5px var(--dark);
  color: rgba(0, 0, 0, .87);
  font-family: sans-serif;
}

h1 { font-family: cursive; }

a {
  font-size: .75rem;
  font-variant: small-caps;
  text-decoration: none;
}

button {
  background: none;
  border: var(--border);
  border-radius: 45px;
  box-shadow: var(--shadow);
  box-sizing: border-box;
  font-size: .75rem;
  font-variant: small-caps;
  padding: .5rem 1rem;
}

.actions {
  align-items: center;
  border-top: var(--border);
  display: flex;
  justify-content: flex-end;
  margin-top: 1rem;
}
.actions > * { margin-left: 1rem;}

.card {
  border: var(--border);
  border-radius: 3px;
  margin-bottom: 1rem;
}
```

```
.card > div { padding: 1rem; }
.card .header {
  background: rgba(0, 0, 0, .87);
  color: rgba(255, 255, 255, .87);
}

/* Layout */
.container {
  column-width: 30rem;
}
```

Figure 5-11. *Theming*

By setting variables, default styles on elements, and creating default container classes, like the `.card` class in Listing 5-9, a theme can be created. Properties one might include in as part of the theme are things that revolve around look and feel such as color, typography, borders, padding, and so on. From there, creating views becomes easier because the primary concern remaining is layout. By setting up default theming, even in a component-based architecture, the look and feel, or brand, can be kept consistent. Furthermore, updating the theme can be as simple as changing the custom property values.

Summary

This chapter covered browser differences and techniques to standardize CSS across them. Techniques for dealing with differences in CSS support in different browsers were also discussed. Finally, theming was addressed. The next chapter will look at supporting user interaction using transitions and animations.

CHAPTER 6

Interactions and Transitions

When we think of HTML and CSS, we often think "static." JavaScript much more commonly comes to mind when thinking of interactions or animations. CSS, however, includes several features that allow for manipulation of elements as a result of user interaction. In this chapter, we will look at how we can respond to user interaction using CSS and how to support those interactions using animations and transitions.

User Interaction Response

One of the most commonly used ways of responding to user interaction in CSS is by using the pseudo elements `:hover`, `:focus`, and `:active`.

The pseudo element `:hover` matches when an element is interacted with using a pointing device – most commonly, when the user hovers with the mouse over the element[1] such as a link or button. This can be used to give the user a visual indication that the element can be interacted with.

The `:focus` pseudo class is triggered when an element receives focus, such as when tabbed to using the keyboard or being clicked. Often overlooked, focus is important as it gives a visual indicator to the user as to which element they are currently interacting with or about to interact with. Changing border styles on an input field when it is in focus will tell the user which field they are about to type in, which is incredibly helpful in orienting the user as to where in the page they are currently at. Not all elements can natively receive focus. Outside of some exceptions such as the video element, buttons, anchor tags, and form items like input and select are the only elements that can receive focus without adding a `tabindex` attribute to the element.

---

[1]:hover. (August 14, 2019). Retrieved from `https://developer.mozilla.org/en-US/docs/Web/CSS/:hover`

© Martine Dowden and Michael Dowden 2020
M. Dowden and M. Dowden, *Architecting CSS*, https://doi.org/10.1007/978-1-4842-5750-0_6

The :active pseudo element triggers when an element is being activated such as a button being pressed or a link being clicked. A change in button style, such as removing a shadow when a physical button is being pressed, reflects real-world expectations of the action of depressing a physical button. Although a user might not be able to articulate why, small interactions such as this will make the interaction feel more natural to the user.

⊛ Accessibility and Focus

Most browsers will have default behavior around elements when focus is applied. If squashing the default behavior, some visual indication of focus needs to be reapplied so that a user can visually distinguish the element that is in focus from other elements.[2] Furthermore, focus should not change the context, functionality, meaning, or operability.[3,4]

From the interaction, a response can then be set such as changing the element's looks, size, or even position. Adding a transition to a visual change, if the animation is informative of the change about to take place, will help the user understand the change being applied. When expanding an accordion for example, animating the opening of the accordion section will help the user stay oriented to where they are in the page especially since content below will be moved to a different location, possibly outside the viewport.

When responding to a CSS-triggered event such as hover, focus, or active, it is much more maintainable to keep the associated transition in CSS as well rather than to use JavaScript. This allows both the trigger and the reaction to stay together and for their association to remain clear and evident. This helps keep visual instructions within the style sheets.

---

[2]Focus Visible. (August 14, 2019). Retrieved from www.w3.org/TR/UNDERSTANDING-WCAG20/navigation-mechanisms-focus-visible.html

[3]Understanding Success Criterion 3.2.1: On Focus. (August 14, 2019). Retrieved from www.w3.org/WAI/WCAG21/Understanding/on-focus.html

[4]Focus Order. (August 14, 2019). Retrieved from www.w3.org/TR/UNDERSTANDING-WCAG20/navigation-mechanisms-focus-order.html

Transform

When creating transitions and animations, although not a requirement, the CSS transform property is often used. Transform allows elements styled with CSS to be transformed in two-dimensional space. Transform functions are based on the transformation matrix. The `matrix()` function is a shorthand for `matrix3d()` which takes six parameters a, b, c, d, tx, and ty, which are shown in bold in Figure 6-1.

$$\begin{bmatrix} \mathbf{a} & \mathbf{c} & 0 & \mathbf{tx} \\ \mathbf{b} & \mathbf{d} & 0 & \mathbf{ty} \\ 0 & 0 & 1 & 0 \\ 0 & 0 & 0 & 1 \end{bmatrix}$$

Figure 6-1. *Transform Matrix*

Parameters a, b, c, and d describe the linear transformation and tx and ty describe the translation to be applied. CSS provides transform functions based on the preceding matrix to manipulate elements such as translate, scale, rotate, skew, and perspective. Using the `translate()` function to change the position of an item, such as sliding something into view, is generally going to be more performant than manipulating its position. The same can be said about `scale()` over changing an element's height or width such as expanding or collapsing a menu or accordion. The `rotate()` function is often used in microanimations; continuing with the accordion example, it can be used to rotate an arrow or caret in the accordion's header to distinguish if the associated panel is open or closed. When the panel is being opened, the arrow can rotate at the same time to inform the user as to the state of the panel in question. Although seemingly insignificant, small details such as this one, if informative, can help the user orient and understand what they are looking at and what is happening. Details regarding the transform functions can be found in Table 6-1.

Table 6-1. *Transform Functions*

Function	Description	Dimension
matrix()	Shorthand for matrix3d(). See the earlier description. Takes six parameters.	2D
matrix3d()	Linear transformation and translation over three dimensions. See the earlier matrix description. Takes 16 values.	3D
translate(tx, ty)	Translation by the vector, where x is the first translation value and y is the second. To individually manipulate the x- or y-axis, translateX(tx) and translateY(ty) can be used.	2D
translate3d(tx, ty, tz)	Same as translate() but on three dimensions. TranslateZ(tz) can be used to translate the element on the z index. This tz value cannot be a percentage, it must be a length.	3D
scale(sx, sy)	Scaling vector, where x scales the height and y scales the width and initial value is 1. To scale the height or width independently, scaleX(sx) and scaleY(sy) can be used.	2D
scale3d()	Same as scale() but on three dimensions. ScaleZ(tz) can be used to translate the element on the z index.	3D
rotate(∠)	Rotates the element from the point of transform-origin by the angle provided.	2D
rotate3d(x, y, z, a)	Rotates an element around a fixed axis in three-dimensional space, where x, y, and z describe the axis of rotation and a describes the angle of rotation.	3D
skew(∠x, ∠y)	Distorts an element by the provided angle on the x- and y-axes. To skew the element by axis, skewX(∠x) and skewY(∠y) can be used.	2D
perspective(z)	Gives perspective to three-dimensional elements where 0 is the default. When z is increased, the element becomes larger, and when it is decreased, the element shrinks.	3D

Transitions

When the styles for an element are changed, transitions allow for the shift from initial state to the new state to be visually smooth. As its name implies, the transition property controls the visual aspect of how values change from one state to another over time.

The transition property is the shorthand property for the following: property, duration, timing function, and delay. Its syntax is described in Listing 6-1 and its properties are defined in Table 6-2.[5]

Listing 6-1. Transition Property Shorthand Syntax

```
transition: property duration timing-function delay;
```

Table 6-2. *Transition Property Values*

Value Name	Behavior	Initial Value
transition -property	Defines the property the transition will affect	all
transition -duration	Defines how long the transition will take to complete	0s
transition -timing -function	Defines the acceleration curb for how the values get applied during the transition	ease
transition -delay	Defines the delay period before the transition starts	0s

Listings 6-2 and 6-3 show an on-hover transition.

---

[5]Transition. (August 15, 2019). Retrieved from `https://developer.mozilla.org/en-US/docs/Web/CSS/transition`

Listing 6-2. HTML for Transition Example

```
<body>
  <a href="">
    <span>Transitions</span>
  </a>
</body>
```

Listing 6-3. CSS for Transition Example

```
html, body {
  padding: 36px;
  margin: 0;
}

a {
  align-items: center;
  background: gray;
  border: solid 1px white;
  color: white;
  display: flex;
  font-size: 36px;
  height: 100px;
  justify-content: center;
  text-decoration: none;
  transition: all 250ms ease-in-out;
}

a:hover {
  background: white;
  border-color: gray;
  color: gray;
  border-radius: 45px;
}
```

In the preceding listing, the link is hovered over causing the background-color, border-color, font color, and border radius to gradually change over 250 milliseconds (see Figure 6-2).

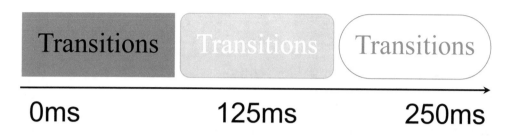

Figure 6-2. *Animation Code Output Over Time*

User Experience   Transitions can be a great way to help guide the user through an application by enhancing the relationship between elements when an action is performed. To achieve this goal, however, the animation should be **informative**, **focused**, and **expressive**.[6] Animations should last between 200 and 500 milliseconds with smaller, less complex animation, or when on a smaller screen, in the 200–300 millisecond range.[7]

Keyframe Animations

Unlike transitions, which can only happen once when the user triggers the event, animations can be repeated over an indefinite period of time. They can also be applied when an element is added to the DOM such as an element going from a `display:none` to `display:block`. This might be the case when opening a menu. The menu items were hidden from the user, and they need to be slid into view rather than abruptly displayed. By animating the display of the menu element, the user implicitly understands the origin of the menu item. Animation also provides more control over the steps of the animation, allowing for much more complexity than in a transition. By percentage along the animation, the keyframe rules set when what changes need to occur. Listings 6-4 and 6-5 show an example using keyframes.

---

[6]Understanding Motion. (August 26, 2016). `https://material.io/design/motion/understanding-motion.html`

[7]Head, Val. How fast should your UI animations be? (August 26, 2019). Retrieved from `https://valhead.com/2016/05/05/how-fast-should-your-ui-animations-be/`

Listing 6-4. Keyframes HTML

```
<body>
  <div class="animations">Animations</div>
</body>
```

Listing 6-5. Keyframes CSS

```
html {
  padding: 0;
  margin: 0;
}

body {
  box-sizing: border-box;
  padding: 36px;
  margin: 0;
}

body > div {
  box-sizing: border-box;
  margin-bottom: 3rem;
}

@keyframes myAnimation {
  0% {
    background: gray;
    border-color: white;
    color: white;
    border-radius: 0px;
    transform: scale(0);
  }
  25% {
    transform: rotate(5deg) scale(.25);
  }
  50% {
    transform: rotate(-10deg) scale(.5);
  }
```

```
  75% {
    transform: rotate(35deg) scale(.75);
  }
  100% {
    background: white;
    border-color: gray;
    color: gray;
    border-radius: 45px;
    transform: rotate(0) scale(1);
  }
}

.animations {
  animation: myAnimation 500ms ease-in-out 1;
  background: white;
  border: solid 1px gray;
  border-radius: 45px;
  box-sizing: border-box;
  color: gray;
  font-size: 2rem;
  padding: 2rem;
  text-align: center;
  width: 100%;
}
```

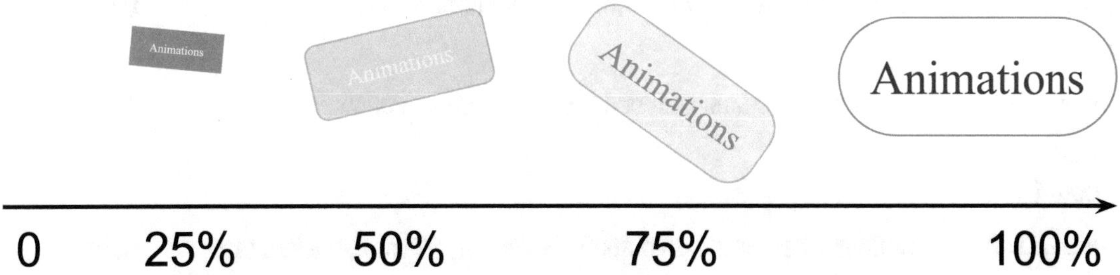

Figure 6-3. *Animation Code Output Over Time*

Background-color, border-color, color, border radius, and scale are only defined at 0 and 100% and are therefore interpolated. The element will rotate to the specified degree at each percent. Even though 100% does not specify a rotation degree, at the end of the animation, the element will set its rotation to what ever is set on the element, or 0.

To trigger the keyframe, the animation property is used (see Listing 6-6). The animation property can take up to seven values: name, duration, timing-function, delay, iteration-count, direction, and fill-mode (details in Table 6-3).

Listing 6-6. Animation Property

```
animation: name duration timing-function delay iteration-count direction
           fill-mode;
```

Table 6-3. *Animation Property Values*

Value Name	Behavior	Initial Value
animation-name	Defines the keyframe at-rule the animation will use	none
animation-duration	Defines how long the animation will take to complete	0s
animation-timing-function	Defines the acceleration curb for how the values get applied during the animation	ease
animation-delay	Defines the delay period before the animation starts	0s
animation-iteration-count	Defines the number of times the animation will play	1
animation-direction	Defines whether the animation should play forward, backward, or toggle forward and backward	normal
animation-fill-mode	Defines how styles are applied to the target before and after animation completes	none

Another property that can be used with animation is `animation-play-state` which allows the developer to pause and start an animation. When resumed, the animation will restart where it was paused rather than the beginning of the sequence. The default value for `animation-play-state` is `running`. It needs to be defined individually as its own property, however, and is not part of the animation shorthand described in Listing 6-4. Giving the user the ability to pause an animation, especially if the animation is not necessary to understanding the content or the state of the application, can radically improve the usability of the application. When considering an auto-advancing carousel, for example, adding the ability to pause the auto-incrementation of panels will allow the user to control the speed at which they view the content.

Animations can also be used when an object is being removed from the DOM, such as when adding a display value of none, but because the `display:none` property will be applied and completed before the animation finishes, this cannot be done with CSS alone. If when closing a menu, `display:none` is added to the menu items, regardless of any animations or transitions set on the elements, the menu will abruptly disappear as the animation will not be given the time to run before the menu items are hidden. To counteract this, the JavaScript `animationend` event is used in conjunction with the CSS to listen to the animation state. `animationend` will trigger upon completion of the animation, at which point `display:none` can be added to the elements which need to be hidden (see Listings 6-7 and 6-8).

Listing 6-7. Animation End Event HTML and JavaScript

```
<body>
  <div class="show-hide">
    <button onclick="toggleAnimation()" id="button">
      Show
    </button>
    <div
      class="animation-container"
      id="animationContainer">
    </div>
  </div>

  <script>
    function showContainer() {
      animationContainer.classList.add('show');
```

```
    }

    function hideContainer() {
      animationContainer.addEventListener('animationend', cleanup);
      animationContainer.classList.replace('show', 'close');
    }

    function cleanup() {
      animationContainer.classList.remove('close');
      animationContainer.removeEventListener('animationend', cleanup);
    }
  </script>
</body>
```

Listing 6-8. Animation End Event CSS

```css
@keyframes roll {
  0%    { transform: translateX(-75vw) rotate(-360deg);  }
  100% { transform: translate(0) rotate(0)}
}

@keyframes roll-reverse {
  0% { transform: translate(0) rotate(0)}
  100%    { transform: translateX(-75vw) rotate(-360deg);  }
}

.animation-container {
  background: linear-gradient(lightgrey, grey);
  border-radius: 50%;
  display: none;
  height: 100px;
  margin: 1rem auto;
  width: 100px;
}

.show {
  display: block;
  animation: roll 1s cubic-bezier(0.280, 0.840, 0.420, 1);
}

.close {
  display: block;
  animation: roll-reverse 1s cubic-bezier(0.280, 0.840, 0.420, 1);
}
```

When the element is "closed" or hidden, first a class with the exit animation is added. Once the animation ends, the `animationend` event listener is triggered and only then can the display property value be changed to none. The same can be achieved with transitions using the `transitionend` event listener. Adding and removing classes, rather than handling the close animation in JavaScript, helps keep display-related logic in the CSS style sheet, increasing maintainability and keeping separation of concerns.

Timing Functions

Whether creating a transition or an animation, a common value to define is the timing function. It determines the speed at which values change over the time it takes for the animation to complete. Timing can help make the animation feel more natural and reflect physical world interactions more closely. When animating a bouncing ball, one would expect the ball to accelerate after hitting the ground. If the animation was linear, and the ball always moved at the same speed, the animation would seem off. There are two specific types of timing functions available.

Easing Functions

Easing functions define smooth transitions based on the Bézier curve, named after the French engineer Pierre Bézier. The curve is parametric,[8] and the cubic variant is defined by four points: P_0, P_1, P_2, and P_3. P_0 and P_3 define the beginning and end of the curve, respectively. P_1 and P_2 represent the control points which give the curve its shape. Each point is defined by (x, y) coordinates.

The CSS `cubic-bezier` predefines P_0 and P_3 at fixed points of $(0, 0)$ and $(1, 1)$ representing the initial and final states of the animation. Left to be defined are P_1 and P_2 whose x values need to remain in a $[0, 1]$ range, while the y values may exist outside of the bounding box.

The CSS function looks as follows: `cubic-bezier(x1, y1, x2, y2)`.

Although the timing can be customized, for convenience CSS includes named common timing functions which include linear, ease, ease-in, ease-in-out, and ease-out (see Table 6-4).

---

[8]Definition of Bézier curve and its properties. (August 29, 2019). Retrieved from `http://web.mit.edu/hyperbook/Patrikalakis-Maekawa-Cho/node12.html`

Table 6-4. *Named Easing Functions[9]*

Name	Formula	Curve
linear	cubic-bezier(0.0, 0.0, 1.0, 1.0)	
ease	cubic-bezier(0.25, 0.1, 0.25, 1.0)	
ease-in	cubic-bezier(0.42, 0.0, 1.0, 1.0)	
ease-in-out	cubic-bezier(0.42, 0.0, 0.58, 1.0)	

(continued)

[9]<timing-function>. (August 29, 2019). Retrieved from https://developer.mozilla.org/en-US/docs/Web/CSS/timing-function

Table 6-4. (*continued*)

Name	Formula	Curve
ease-out	`cubic-bezier(0.42, 0.0, 0.58, 1.0)`	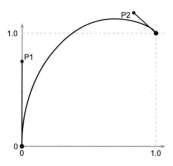

To create bouncing effects, either or both y values should be set outside the [0, 1] range. For this, a custom function needs to be written such as in the following function: `cubic-bezier(0, 0.71, 0.64, 1.23)`.

The curve is plotted in Figure 6-4.

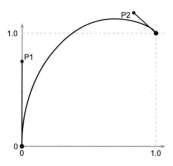

Figure 6-4. *Sample Bounce Curve*

Stepping Functions

Although not currently well supported across browsers, instead of a curve, a stepping function which divides the animation into equal segments across time can also be used. Two values are used to define the animation's timing: number of steps (n) and step position (see Table 6-5). The syntax is as follows:

```
animation-timing-function: steps(n, step-position);
```

Table 6-5. *Named Stepping Functions[10]*

Name	Function	Steps
step-start	steps(1, start)	
step-end	steps(1, end)	
jump-start	steps(3, jump-start)	
jump-end	steps(3, jump-end)	

(continued)

---

[10]<timing-function>. (August 29, 2019). Retrieved from https://developer.mozilla.org/en-US/docs/Web/CSS/timing-function

Table 6-5. (*continued*)

Name	Function	Steps
jump-none	step(3, jump-none)	
jump-both	step(3, jump-both)	

When applied, the code and output would be as in Listings 6-9 and 6-10 and Figure 6-5.

Listing 6-9. jump-start Sample Code HTML

```
<body>
  <div class="jump-start">jump-start</div>
</body>
```

Listing 6-10. jump-start Sample Code CSS

```
body {
  box-sizing: border-box;
  padding: 36px;
  margin: 0;
}

body > div {
  box-sizing: border-box;
```

```
  margin-bottom: 3rem;
}

@keyframes jumpStart {
 0% {
    width: 0;
    background-color: white;
    border: 1px solid gray;
 }
 100% {
    width: 90vw;
    background-color: gray;
    border: 1px solid gray;
 }
}
.jump-start {
  animation-name: jumpStart;
  animation-duration: 5s;
  animation-iteration-count: infinite;
  margin-bottom: 4px;
  animation-timing-function: steps(5, jump-start);
}
```

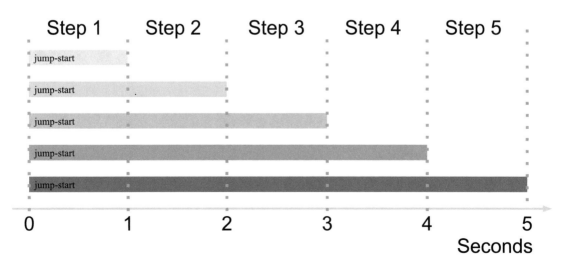

Figure 6-5. *Jump-Start Output*

Notice how the animation is already partially started. Because jump-start is used, the initial state of width 0 and color white is skipped and the animation starts with the container at a width of 20% of final state width. If jump-end had been used, the container would have started at a width of 0, but never reached a width of 100%. The container would only have a width of 80% when the animation ended.

⊛ Accessibility and Timing

When considering timing, it is important to make sure that the content does not flash more than three times in a one-second period. This is to prevent the induction of seizures due to photosensitivity in users.[11]

Performance Considerations

When considering the effects of animations on performance, not all animations are created equal. Animations that cause layout changes or the view to be repainted are particularly taxing.[12] For example, changes to height, width, or position affect layout and cause elements on the page to be repositioned. Properties that cause the view to repaint include color, background-position, and visibility. Animations affecting layout and paint will be less performant than those that don't.

Generally, for best performance, using the transform property is the best way to go as it can lean on the GPU. Whenever possible, it is best to try and stick to animation using opacity, translate, rotate, and scale.[13]

When performance issues do arise, it can be tempting to use the will-change property. Will-change informs the browser ahead of time of the changes that will be animated, allowing the browser to optimize for them; however, when misused, it can do more harm than good. Some guidelines to the proper use of will-change include the following:

---

[11]Web Content Accessibility Guidelines (WCAG 2.1). (August 31, 2019). www.w3.org/TR/WCAG21

[12]Animations and Performance. (August 31, 2019). Retrieved from https://developers.google.com/web/fundamentals/design-and-ux/animations/animations-and-performance

[13]High Performance Animations. (August 31, 2019). Retrieved from www.html5rocks.com/en/tutorials/speed/high-performance-animations/

- **Sparse use** – It should only be used when it is actually needed. The browser already attempts to optimize everything. Unnecessary use will actually slow down the page.

- **Only on when needed** – Should be turned on before the animation will trigger and then turned off again to free up browser resources being used for optimization.

- **Enough time** – Optimization is time-consuming; therefore, `will-change` needs to be applied to the element with enough time to take effect before the animation is set to begin.[14]

Summary

This chapter covered transition, animations, and their differences as well as the functions used to change the timing of how animations and transforms are applied. Also covered were performance and accessibility considerations when dealing with animations. Chapter 7 will go over preprocessors and their architecture considerations and benefits.

---

[14]CSS Will Change Module Level 1. (August 31, 2019). Retrieved from `www.w3.org/TR/css-will-change-1/`

Preprocessors

For CSS there are several preprocessors available. These will take data, written in their own particular syntax, and then output CSS for the browser to consume. The benefit of these includes access to functionality such as color-editing functions or nesting rules that are not yet available in CSS. They also gave us access to CSS variables before they were supported by the language itself. Some of the most popular processors include Sass, Less, and Stylus.

Note   Examples in this chapter will use SCSS.[1] These techniques are available using other preprocessors; however, feature availability and syntax will vary based on the preprocessor used.

Implications for Architecture

The way in which code is organized and architected can be very different when using preprocessors than when using pure CSS because of added functionality, such as mixins and the ability to extend classes. The ability to compute values in ways simply not available outside of preprocessors today brings the ability to write DRY semantic code. It can be defined in just one place and then reused throughout the style sheet not much differently than some of the object-oriented principles used in other programming languages.

The downside of using preprocessors is that they add a layer of complexity to the application that does not exist when using pure CSS. Even though some preprocessors, such as Less,[2] can be run in the browser directly, it is not recommended for production use because it is less performant and reliable than plain CSS. When using preprocessors, we therefore need some sort of build step in order to compile the code into CSS.

---

[1]https://sass-lang.com/documentation/syntax
[2]http://lesscss.org/usage/#using-less-in-the-browser

© Martine Dowden and Michael Dowden 2020
M. Dowden and M. Dowden, *Architecting CSS*, https://doi.org/10.1007/978-1-4842-5750-0_7

Debugging can also be a challenge, especially when using some of the more complex or advanced features of the code. This stems from the CSS being generated not matching one-to-one with the code being written. For example, the properties and attributes being added to a class could come from a mixin (more about mixins later in this chapter) rather than part of the ruleset. The CSS being applied is the output, not the mixin itself, so tracking back to which mixin created the output can be difficult. Sourcemaps can help with this. A sourcemap is a file that can be generated with the CSS which links the output back to the code that generated it. But again, this needs to be set up specifically as part of the build process.

So first, before even choosing the processor to be used, the question of whether the added complexity is necessary should be asked.

Nesting

Nesting allows us to have a clear visual hierarchy, which CSS does not have. The following CSS (Listing 7-1) can be nested (Listing 7-2), making it evident at a glance what the hierarchy is.

Listing 7-1. CSS

```
nav {
  padding: 0;
  margin: 0;
}
nav ul {
  padding: 0;
}
nav ul li {
  padding: 10px;
  border: solid 1px blue;
  background: yellow;
  color: yellow;
}
```

Listing 7-2. Nested SCSS

```scss
nav {
  padding: 0;
  margin: 0;
  ul {
    padding: 0;
    li {
      padding: 10px;
      border: solid 1px blue;
      background: yellow;
      color: blue;
    }
  }
}
```

As much as it makes it very easy to know that the styles set on the list item will only be applied to the navigation list items, nesting makes it really easy to create overly specific rules. In the preceding example, nesting the list item inside of the unordered list is superfluous and does not add any value. Having it nested under the navigation only, one level higher than its current location, would be sufficient.

Nesting can, however, bring clarity to some situations. Let's look at Listing 7-3.

Listing 7-3. Nested SCSS

```scss
a:link, a:visited {
  color: gray;
  font-variant: small-caps;
  border: dotted 1px rgba(0, 0, 0, 0);
  text-decoration: none;
  &:hover { border: dotted 1px cornflowerblue; }
  &:focus { border: solid 1px cadetblue; }
  &:active { border: double 1px darkcyan; }
}
```

The ampersand refers back to the parent element, so the hover is placed on the anchor tag when it is a link, or a visited link. Nesting here makes it very clear that the hover, focus, and active selectors are all children of a:link and a:visited.

Without nesting, the code would have looked something like this (Listing 7-4):

Listing 7-4. Nonnested CSS

```
a:link,
a:visited {
  color: gray;
  font-variant: small-caps;
  border: dotted 1px rgba(0, 0, 0, 0);
  text-decoration: none;
}
a:link:hover,
a:visited:hover {
  border: dotted 1px cornflowerblue;
}
a:link:focus,
a:visited:focus {
  border: solid 1px cadetblue;
}
a:link:active,
a:visited:active {
  border: double 1px darkcyan;
}
```

Without nesting, it is more difficult to tell at a glance that links and visited links also have styles for hover, focus, and active states. Furthermore, the nested code is more concise and does not repeat the root elements, decreasing the chance of typos or errors.

Care when nesting must be taken in order not to create rules that are overly specific. This happens when elements are nested too deep. However, it can help with code legibility.

Color Functions and Variables

Variables, although available today in CSS as discussed in Chapter 2, were first made available through the use of preprocessors. The CSS version (custom properties), although influenced by preprocessor variables, does have some advantages over the preprocessor variables. Custom properties can be accessed and changed via JavaScript, while preprocessor variables cannot. In creating the CSS output, preprocessor variables do not remain variables; they are replaced by their assigned value. CSS custom properties, however, stay variables and can be manipulated at any time, including during runtime.

Although variables can be used for any value, such as default padding amount, they are extremely powerful when used in conjunction with color functions to define the theme of an application. The brand colors for an application include those given in Table 7-1.

Table 7-1. *Color Values and Usage*

Color	Name	Hex	Usage
	Medium Taupe	#AEC5EB	Primary
	Pastel Pink	#E9AFA3	Accent
	Pale Cornflower Blue	#AEC5EB	Links
	Unbleached Silk	#F9DEC9	Background
	Charcoal	#3A405A	Text & default gray

The colors can be set to semantic names based upon what their usage will be and then manipulated using color functions when the color value or saturation needs to be altered (Listing 7-1).

Color functions will vary based on the preprocessor used; most include functions to lighten, darken, or shift the hue, saturation, or transparency of a color. In Listing 7-5, we use scale-color() which takes a color and then can alter any combination of the following color properties: red, green blue, saturation, lightness, and alpha. When setting lightness to 10%, we are making the color 10% lighter than the original and keeping all other values the same.

Listing 7-5. Colors

```
$primary: #AEC5EB;
$accent: #E9AFA3;
$links: #AEC5EB;
$background: #F9DEC9;
$dark: #3A405A;
$light: #FAFAFA;
```

```
$border: solid 1px $light;
$dark-text: $dark;
$light-text: $light;

$spacing: 1.25rem;

body {
  background: scale-color($background, $lightness: 10%);
  color: $dark-text;
  padding: $spacing;
}
a:link, a:visited {
  color: $link;
}
a:hover, a:focus {
  color: scale-color($link, $lightness: -10%);
}
button {
  color: $light-text;
  background: $primary;
  border: $border;
  padding: $spacing;
}
section, article {
  background: scale-color($background, $lightness: 20%);
  padding: $spacing;
  margin-bottom: $spacing;
}
```

By using color transformation functions and variables, not only don't we have to remember the exact values for each of the colors and any variations we may have in use, but we also increase our ability to keep our theme consistent. Furthermore, if the colors were to change, this could be done in one place. The eventuality of a color changing is why color names should be based upon their usage rather than their actual color. If the variable name was $pink, for example, and the accent color was changed to purple, we would now have to either find the variable name everywhere and update it, or we would have a variable name that does not represent the color that is assigned to it. Situations like this make maintainability very difficult and code confusing. Selecting semantic variable names is incredibly important to the maintainability of the code.

Mixins

Mixins allow developers to create sets of properties and values that can easily be reused throughout the application.

Simple Mixin

The simple example shown in Listing 7-6 shows the use of a simple mixin to define a set of properties in one place and then include them in another context. The `@include` property is used to assign the previously defined mixin to the new context – an element in this case – but it could just as easily be included within a class definition.

Listing 7-6. Simple Mixin

```
@mixin card {
  background: white;
  box-sizing: border-box;
  margin-bottom: 1rem;
  padding: 1rem;
  box-shadow: 1px 1px 3px silver
}

div {
  @include card;
}
```

Parameters

Mixins can also take parameters in order to change the outputs of the mixin based on the parameters passed, as shown with the `$elevation` parameter in Listing 7-7.

Listing 7-7. Mixin with Arguments

```
@mixin card($elevation) {
  background: white;
  box-sizing: border-box;
  margin-bottom: 1rem;
  padding: 1rem;

  $offset: $elevation * 1;
  $blur: $elevation * 2;
  box-shadow: #{$offset}px #{$offset}px #{$blur}px silver;
}

div {
  @include card(3);
}
```

Arguments

Logic can also be added within the mixin. In Listing 7-8, styles are applied differently based upon a non-zero $elevation.

Listing 7-8. Mixin with Arguments and Logic

```
@mixin card($elevation) {
  background: white;
  box-sizing: border-box;
  margin-bottom: 1rem;
  padding: 1rem;

  @if $elevation == 0 {
    border: solid 1px silver;
  } @else {
    $offset: $elevation * 1;
    $blur: $elevation * 2;
    box-shadow: #{$offset}px #{$offset}px #{$blur}px silver;
  }
}
```

```
body {
  padding: 2rem;
}
h1 {
  margin: 0;
}
header {
  @include card(0)
}
div {
  @include card(2);
}
```

The advantage of using mixins, especially with arguments, is that it allows for DRY code. The code is written once and managed in one place but applied to multiple classes. The preceding code (Listing 7-8) would compile to what is shown in Listing 7-9 and display Figure 7-1.

Listing 7-9. CSS Output

```
body {
  padding: 2rem;
}

h1 {
  margin: 0;
}

header {
  background: white;
  box-sizing: border-box;
  margin-bottom: 1rem;
  padding: 1rem;
  border: solid 1px silver;
}
```

```
div {
  background: white;
  box-sizing: border-box;
  margin-bottom: 1rem;
  padding: 1rem;
  box-shadow: 2px 2px 4px silver;
}
```

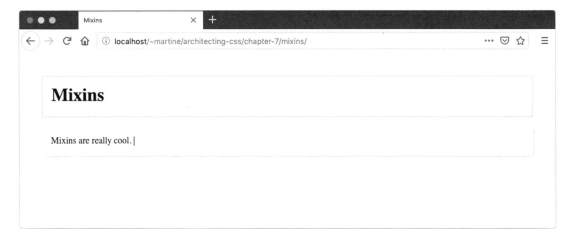

Figure 7-1. *Mixins Output*

Mixins are very powerful in preventing the need to duplicate code or nonsemantic class names. Without mixins, the earlier code would require a potentially infinite number of classes, or have to rewrite the border and shadow multiple times and then maintain it in multiple locations. Another great application is when a specific parameter might apply to many aspects of an element, but differs depending on context, while the rest of the element needs to stay consistent regardless of the situation. Informational boxes to the user might be an example, where there is a need for information, successes, warnings, and errors. The boxes need to look the same except for color (Listings 7-10 and 7-11 and Figure 7-2).

Listing 7-10. Informational Boxes HTML

```
<body>
  <p class="message info">Information</p>
  <p class="message success">Success</p>
```

```
  <p class="message warning">Warning</p>
  <p class="message error">Error</p>
</body>
```

Listing 7-11. Informational Boxes SCSS

```scss
@mixin message($color) {
  background: lighten($color, 40%);
  border: solid 1px $color;
}

body {
  padding: 2rem;
}

.message {
  padding: 1rem;
}

.info {
  @include message(blue);
}

.success {
  @include message(green);
}

.warning {
  @include message(orange);
}

.error {
  @include message(red);
}
```

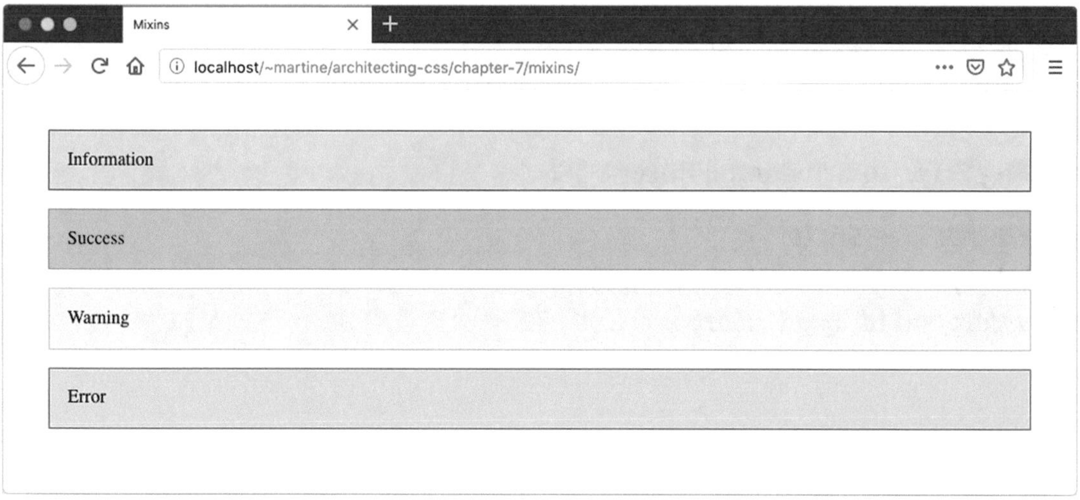

Figure 7-2. *Informational Boxes*

Even though the padding could have been included in the mixin, it is separated out into its own class because when a mixin is added, it does its computation and outputs all the code each time; therefore, mixins are not a good use case for static information. Static styles are simply programmatically being copied over into each class increasing the size of the CSS and therefore upload time. Classes, defaults on elements, or the use of the @extend at-rule are much better options for static styles.

@extend

Extend, unlike mixins, prevents the duplication of code in the resulting CSS. While a mixin copies the declaration block for each selector it is included within, extend creates a single declaration block and consolidates the selectors.

The advantage of this methodology is in creating base classes for basic styles toward which semantically named classes will be pointed. The code is neither duplicated nor copied and prevents the use of numerous nonsemantic classes on an HTML element. For code maintainability it also means that the style of the elements is controlled in the CSS. If the style coming from extending another rule is no longer wanted, we need only to remove the @extend. By simply adding the class name to the HTML instead of using @extend, we would have had to edit the HTML in order to change look and feel. By using @extend instead of adding the same class name to a multitude of elements, we continue to maintain a separation of concerns. Our elements can have class names that match their purpose, rather than how they display, and we handle the styling via the CSS.

Revisiting the example found in the "Mixins" section rather than adding both message and the type to each class, we can create one class that determines the type and has the defaults set by .message (see Listings 7-12 and 7-13 and Figure 7-3).

Listing 7-12. Informational Boxes HTML – Revisited

```
<body>
  <p class="info-message">Information</p>
  <p class="success-message">Success</p>
  <p class="warning-message">Warning</p>
  <p class="error-message">Error</p>
</body>
```

Listing 7-13. Informational Boxes SCSS – Revisited

```
@mixin message($color) {
  background: lighten($color, 40%);
  border: solid 1px $color;
}

body {
  padding: 2rem;
}

.message {
  padding: 1rem;
}

.info-message {
  @include message(blue);
  @extend .message;
}

.success-message {
  @include message(green);
  @extend .message
}
```

```
.warning-message {
  @include message(orange);
  @extend .message
}

.error-message {
  @include message(red);
  @extend .message
}
```

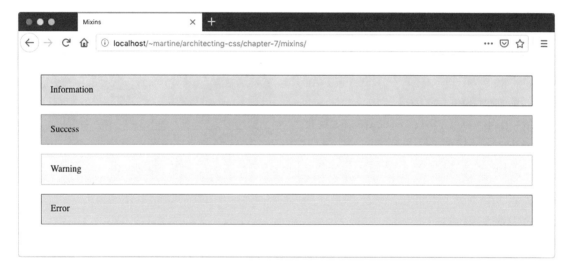

Figure 7-3. *Informational Boxes – Revisited*

Notice both examples have the same resulting appearance. But the latter allows for only having one class dictating the entire class for the element rather than two. For code maintainability, the power of @extend lies in the ability to declare the entire class in one place without copy-pasting or duplicating the code both in the Sass and also in the compiled CSS (see Listing 7-14 for the CSS output).

Listing 7-14. Informational Boxes – Revisited Output CSS

```
body {
  padding: 2rem;
}
```

```
.message, .error-message, .warning-message, .success-message, .info-message {
  padding: 1rem;
}

.info-message {
  background: #ccccff;
  border: solid 1px blue;
}

.success-message {
  background: #4dff4d;
  border: solid 1px green;
}

.warning-message {
  background: #ffedcc;
  border: solid 1px orange;
}

.error-message {
  background: #ffcccc;
  border: solid 1px red;
}
```

Notice the message class now has multiple other selectors as well, but was not duplicated in the output.

@Import

Imports allow the user to create partial files in which variables, mixins, and reusable code can be placed. Sass imports work similarly to CSS imports in that it copies the SCSS they contain to the style sheet they are being imported by. They must therefore be used with caution. It is very easy to bloat code by repeatedly importing an entire theme, for example, into each component. Sharing mixins and variables, since they are not copied, but produce an output within a style, is a perfect application of the use of @import, because unlike classes, they do not get copied.

Creating import files to have information accessible from anywhere in the application becomes very interesting when dealing with components because more often than not, such as when using Angular out of the box or creating component in JavaScript and Shadow DOM, the CSS is scoped and therefore in a separate file or area of the application than the rest of the CSS. Adding variables and mixins to a **partial** – a file to be imported into other files that do not have a use on its own – helps keep the code DRY.

Note   Partials are sometimes denoted by having an underscore at the beginning of their name to separate them from style sheets.

Another use case of `@import` is to prevent an application's CSS style sheet from becoming an unmaintainable megalith of a file. By breaking the CSS into smaller sections to be imported into a main style sheet, the code can be easier to find, collaborate on, and maintain (see Listing 7-15).

Listing 7-15. `@import`

```
@import "_variables"
@import "nav"
@import "carousel"
    .
    .
    .
a:link, a:visited { ... }
    .
    .
    .
```

Summary

In this chapter we looked at a very small subset of functionality brought to use via the use of preprocessors. We looked at mixins, imports, extends, color function, and variable and how they impact how we might organize and structure our application's CSS. In the next chapter, we will look at how JavaScript can interact with our CSS especially in the context of modern frameworks.

CHAPTER 8

Frameworks, Libraries, and JavaScript

In a real-world application, your CSS does not function in isolation. This chapter covers some of the important considerations of a modern front-end web application, including how your choice of CSS or JavaScript frameworks may impact your application styles.

JavaScript

OK, yes this is a CSS book, so why are we suddenly talking about JavaScript? The reality is that a significant amount of front-end development is done using some sort of framework and/or UI library, many of which rely on JavaScript. Furthermore, JavaScript is often used to manipulate CSS as a result of state change or user interaction.

According to Stack Overflow's 2019 annual survey, the most popular programming language for the past seven consecutive years is JavaScript. The breakdown of the top ten can be found in Figure 8-1.[1]

---

[1]Developer Survey Results 2019. (2019). Retrieved from Focus Visible. (August 14, 2019). Retrieved on October 29, 2019, from `https://insights.stackoverflow.com/survey/2019#technology`

© Martine Dowden and Michael Dowden 2020
M. Dowden and M. Dowden, *Architecting CSS*, https://doi.org/10.1007/978-1-4842-5750-0_8

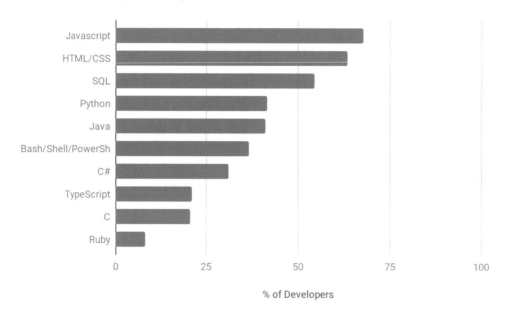

Figure 8-1. *Most Popular Programming, Scripting, and Markup Languages in 2019 According to Stack Overflow*

The most popular web framework is still jQuery, followed by React and Angular. The top ten breakdown is shown in Figure 8-2.[2]

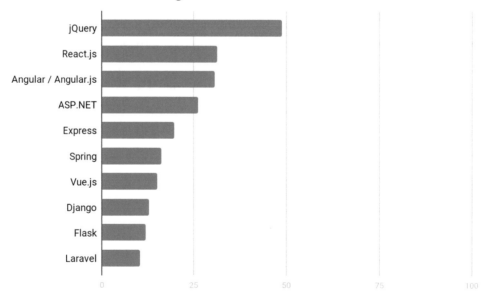

Figure 8-2. *Most Popular Web Frameworks in 2019 According to Stack Overflow*

---

[2]Developer Survey Results 2019. (2019). Retrieved from Focus Visible. (August 14, 2019). Retrieved on October 29, 2019, from https://insights.stackoverflow.com/survey/2019#technology

Manipulating CSS Using JS

Made easy by libraries such as jQuery, and vanilla JavaScript properties such as element.ClassList, we have been manipulating our CSS via our JS for years. But what exactly does that do to specificity and cascading? Table 8-1 lists some of the common ways of affecting visual output through JS and their impact on specificity.

Table 8-1. *CSS Altering JavaScript Methods*

Property and Methods	What It Does	Effects on Specificity
element.ClassList • add() • remove() • replace() • toggle() • item() • contains()	Reads and manipulates the classes attached to a particular element.	Because styles are being applied by referencing classes, cascading and inheritance will not be significantly impacted.
element.style *Examples:* elem.style = "color: blue, font-size: 12px" *Or* elem. setAttribute("style", "color:blue; font-size: 12px" *Or* elem.style.color = "blue"	Adds styles inline on the element.	Very difficult to override because they are inline. If the element already has inline styles, they will be overridden by what is being applied by the JavaScript.

Both a huge advantage and risk, JavaScript has the ability to easily override anything declared by CSS but does not have to.

If we don't want to mix CSS rules in our JavaScripts, the methods given to us via classList allow for adding and removing classes to the element without ever touching the CSS itself. This brings with it the huge benefit of styling definition staying in CSS files and not being split between JS and CSS files.

Affecting styles or the DOM itself brings the advantage that the specificity of CSS being applied matters very little since it will be overridden. Via this technique, regardless of any other context, as a developer, we can dictate that if a user performs a certain action, or a particular state is achieved, a particular set of styles will be applied regardless of other styling, or context. This technique is often used to show and hide dialog boxes, for example, notification messages. The advantage of this technique is that the style changes can stay with its trigger, or action, and regardless of context, the styles being applied will not be overridden by preexisting CSS.

There are situations where JavaScript allows us to do things that are simply not possible with pure HTML and CSS solution. A perfect example would be using event listeners for the animation's timing, start, or end (see Listings 8-1 to 8-3 and Figure 8-3).

Listing 8-1. Animation Listener HTML

```
<body>
  <div class="image">
    <img src="art.png" alt="modern art" id="image">
    <button onClick="rotateImage()" id="button">Rotate Image</button>
  </div>
</body>
```

Listing 8-2. Animation Listener CSS

```
html, body {
  padding: 36px;
  margin: 0;
}

@keyframes rotate {
  0% { transform: rotate(0deg); }
  100% { transform: rotate(360deg); }
}
.rotate { animation: rotate ease-in-out 500ms 1; }
```

```css
.image { text-align: center; }
img { max-width: 100%; }
button {
  display: block;
  margin: 1rem auto;
  padding: 1rem;
  width: 25%;
}
```

Listing 8-3. Animation Listener JavaScript

```javascript
var image, button;

(function() {
  'use strict';
  image = document.getElementById('image');
  image.addEventListener('animationend', reEnableButton);
  button = document.getElementById('button');
})();

function reEnableButton() {
  button.disabled = false;
  image.classList.remove('rotate');
}

function rotateImage() {
  image.classList.add('rotate');
  button.disabled = true;
}
```

Figure 8-3. *Animation Listener Output*

The button triggers the JavaScript to disable the button and add a class of rotate which makes the image spin once. Because on page load, we set up the JavaScript to listen for animation's ending, once the animation is terminated, we can reset the page. The button is reenabled, and the rotate class is removed. In this example, even though we are manipulating the CSS with JavaScript, the CSS classes are still defined and maintained in the CSS file, and therefore, inheritance and cascading are not altered or affected.

Component-Based Architecture

When using component-based architecture, it becomes very important not only to theme your application to your application's brand/specification, but also the UI library itself. Each library will have various levels of themability and intricacies in terms of ease, as well as what is actually possible to style. When selecting a UI library, understanding the customizability and how themable a library or framework is can save you from a lot of headaches down the road. **Encapsulation** – restricting the component CSS to the component itself – allows for writing CSS that only applies to a particular component and not to the rest of the application. If a UI library's components has very strict encapsulation and few theming options, it will be incredibly difficult to style.

There are many different libraries and frameworks that create or use components. Each has slightly different implementations. We are not going to look at all of them. When looking at how modern-day JavaScript frameworks create and interact with components, most either use web components or emulate them. Worth noting is that especially if the component is emulated, it will behave slightly differently than what I will be describing in the following text. Angular has an emulated model and continues to support an equivalent shadow piercing combinator (::ng-deep) but can be set to use web components instead, or set to have no encapsulation at all. In React, it depends on how the CSS was set up in the project. The options also run the gamut. Understanding exactly how much encapsulation your framework provides will help make better decisions as to how to structure your CSS.

Libraries and Frameworks

By definition, libraries are collections of declarations that the application will use. A framework is an abstraction and provides basic functionality, or a skeleton for the application. A framework may contain one or more libraries.

UI libraries such as jQuery UI[3] or Angular Material[4] provide a series of components or widgets that can be added to an application. They come ready made with styles and functionality. To customize their looks, they need to be themed. Theming can either be done via tools, which spit out the necessary CSS such as themerollers, or be done more manually following guidelines. Either way, the themability and therefore customizability of the said library will vary. The variability is a direct result of how the components are constructed and how easy the author has made it for element to be customized. Further customization beyond what the theme will allow can often prove quite difficult and result in using extremely specific selectors, such as the use of `!important`. It is therefore very important, when considering libraries, to look into what theming capabilities it has as well as how easy it is going to be to customize so its elements can match your application.

The architecture of the library itself may also affect how it is used and in some cases may provide for multiple approaches. Bootstrap[5] is interesting because its structure allows for two radically different implementations, each with their downfalls and benefits.

The first, and probably most common implementation, is importing both the CSS and JavaScript directly in the page, from a local source, via CDN, or using a package manager such as NPM, NuGet, or RubyGems. The framework in its entirety is available and being applied. This means that a number of classes already have styles added to them and are ready to use on the web site. Some components, like modals, have functionality that relies on JavaScript associated with them. These will also be readily available.

The drawbacks of this approach lie in three places:

1. Naming is no longer semantic.

2. The styles are essentially being controlled by the HTML.

3. Everything is imported in its entirety even if it's not being used.

---

[3] https://jqueryui.com/

[4] https://material.angular.io/

[5] https://getbootstrap.com/

Consider a static web site with three pages using the same basic layout for all three of its pages. The layout contains one main section and an aside to the right of the main (see Listings 8-4 and 8-5 and Figure 8-4).

Listing 8-4. Bootstrap HTML

```html
<!DOCTYPE html>
<html lang="en">
<head>
  <title>Bootstrap</title>
  <meta charset="UTF-8">

  <!-- bootstrap -->
  <link rel="stylesheet" href="https://stackpath.bootstrapcdn.com/
  bootstrap/4.3.1/css/bootstrap.min.css" integrity="sha384-ggOyR0iXCbMQv3Xip
  ma34MD+dH/1fQ784/j6cY/iJTQUOhcWr7x9JvoRxT2MZw1T" crossorigin="anonymous">
</head>

<body class="container">
  <h1>Food</h1>

  <div class="row">
    <main class="col-md-9">
      <div class="jumbotron">
        <h2>Yum</h2>
        <p>Gummi bears chocolate bar powder brownie… </p>
        <button class="btn btn-warning">Call To Action</button>
      </div>
      <h2 id="cupcakes">Cupcakes</h2>
      <p>Chocolate chocolate bar tart cookie chocolate… </p>
      <a class="btn btn-light">Read More</a>
    </main>
    <aside id="bacon" class="col-md-3">
      <h2>Bacon</h2>
      <p>Bacon ipsum dolor amet pork loin chicken ham… </p>
      <p>Jowl spare ribs turkey cupim, pork chop sirloin… </p>
      <a class="btn btn-light">Read More</a>
    </aside>
  </div>
```

```
<!-- Bootstrap scripts -->
<script src="https://code.jquery.com/jquery-3.3.1.slim.min.js"
integrity="sha384-q8i/X+965DzO0rT7abK41JStQIAqVgRVzpbzo5smXKp4YfRvH+8abtT
E1Pi6jizo" crossorigin="anonymous"></script>
<script src="https://cdnjs.cloudflare.com/ajax/libs/popper.js/1.14.7/umd/
popper.min.js" integrity="sha384-UO2eT0CpHqdSJQ6hJty5KVphtPhzWj9WO1clHTMG
a3JDZwrnQq4sF86dIHNDz0W1" crossorigin="anonymous"></script>
<script src="https://stackpath.bootstrapcdn.com/bootstrap/4.3.1/js/
bootstrap.min.js" integrity="sha384-JjSmVgyd0p3pXB1rRibZUAYoIIy6OrQ6VrjIE
aFf/nJGzIxFDsf4x0xIM+BO7jRM" crossorigin="anonymous"></script>

</body>
</html>
```

Listing 8-5. Bootstrap CSS

```
html, body {
  padding: 36px;
  margin: 0;
}
```

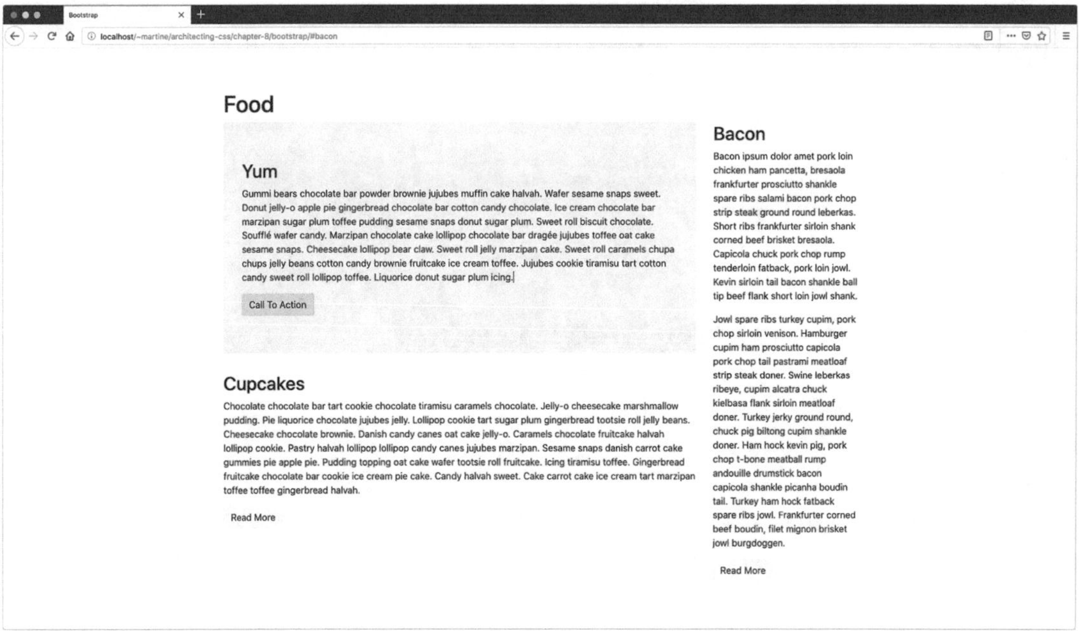

Figure 8-4. *Bootstrap Output*

The benefit of this approach is its simplicity. Either with a custom theme, or just using defaults such as in the earlier example, it is very fast to get up and running. A number of basic styles already exist and can be used to just create a layout. The big downfall is in the maintainability of the code. Keeping consistency becomes very difficult if there are multiple call to action buttons across multiple pages.

```
<button class="btn btn-warning">Call To Action</button>
```

If the btn or the btn-warning class is updated, all buttons that include this generic class across the application will be updated, whether a call to action or not. The class gives no indication of what it might be used for, or worse, such as in this example, it is being used because of its color, rather than for a warning. The only other option is to go find all the call to actions in the application and update their class name.

Rather than the style sheet controlling how elements look, the style is now tightly bound to the HTML. This is also true of the layout, wanting to change the aside to taking a third of the page rather than a quarter would involve going to each page, and updating the HTML.

The other option is to take advantage of the available Sass mixins that Bootstrap makes available (see Listings 8-6 and 8-7).

Listing 8-6. Bootstrap Mixins HTML

```
<!DOCTYPE html>
<html lang="en">

<head>
  <title>Bootstrap</title>
  <meta charset="UTF-8">
  <!-- Application CSS -->
  <link rel="stylesheet" href="./styles.css">
</head>

<body>
  <h1>Food</h1>
  <div class="container">
    <main>
      <div class="call-to-action">
        <h2>Yum</h2>
```

```html
    <p>Gummi bears chocolate bar powder brownie… </p>
    <button>Call To Action</button>
  </div>
  <h2>Cupcakes</h2>
  <p>Chocolate chocolate bar tart cookie chocolate… </p>
  <a class="read-more">Read More</a>
</main>
<aside>
  <h2>Bacon</h2>
  <p>Bacon ipsum dolor amet pork loin chicken ham pancetta… </p>
  <a class="read-more">Read More</a>
</aside>
  </div>
</body>
</html>
```

Listing 8-7. Bootstrap Mixins SCSS

```scss
@import './node_modules/bootstrap/scss/functions';
@import './node_modules/bootstrap/scss/variables';
@import './node_modules/bootstrap/scss/mixins';

@import './node_modules/bootstrap/scss/jumbotron';
@import './node_modules/bootstrap/scss/buttons';

html {
  padding: 36px;
}

body {
  padding: 36px 15px;
  margin: 0 auto;
  font-family: -apple-system,BlinkMacSystemFont,"Segoe UI",Roboto,
  "Helvetica Neue",Arial,"Noto Sans",sans-serif,"Apple Color Emoji",
  "Segoe UI Emoji","Segoe UI Symbol","Noto Color Emoji";
  font-weight: 400;
  line-height: 1.5;
  color: #212529;
```

```scss
  box-sizing: border-box;
}

h1, h2 {
  margin-top: 0;
  margin-bottom: .5rem;
  font-weight: 500;
  line-height: 1.2;
}
h1 { font-size: 2.5rem ;}
h2 { font-size: 2rem ;}

.container {
  box-sizing: border-box;
  @include make-row(15px);
  & > * {
    box-sizing: border-box;
    @include make-col-ready(1rem);
  }
}

button { @extend .btn }
.call-to-action {
  box-sizing: border-box;
  @extend .jumbotron;
  button {
    @include button-variant($yellow, $yellow);
  }
}
a.read-more {
  @extend .btn;
  @include button-variant($gray-100, $gray-100);
}

@media (min-width: 756px) {
  body {  max-width: 540px; }
}
```

```scss
@media (min-width: 768px) {
  body {  max-width: 720px; }
  main { @include make-col(9); }
  aside { @include make-col(3) }
}

@media (min-width: 992px) {
  body {  max-width: 960px; }
}

@media (min-width: 1200px) {
  body {  max-width: 1140px; }
}
```

This approach is not going to be as easy to get up and running with. Since it uses SCSS, it will require the ability to process SCSS into CSS. Knowledge of SCSS and of what is available for mixins in the framework is also required. Once past the setup and learning curve, however, we get some great benefits. Because we are now assigning the styles to classes via @include and @extend instead of applying generic class names to elements in the HTML, we know our elements will look the same on all the pages. Elements across the entire application can also be updated from one place rather than searching the site for all instances of a particular concept. Lastly, only the parts of Bootstrap I am using are being imported which reduces page weight.

!Important   Whenever trying to theme a component library or tweaking the styles from a CSS framework, specificity can sometimes be challenging to wrangle, as the library or framework may already be using selectors that are quite specific; therefore, it may be tempting to use !important. Here be Dragons!

Although there are situations where there truly is no other choice, or important truly is the lesser evil, these instances are few and far between.

The use of !important increases the precedence of a declaration making it very difficult to overide or to include in a normal cascade. No longer can you target a more specific selector to change the style of the element. You now need another more specific important. This vicious cycle makes code incredibly difficult to debug and maintain and even harder to expand.

So when overriding styles, take care that if you do use `!important`, it is done sparingly and with intent rather than frustration.

Knowing the architecture of the library selected, and its capabilities, will help make informed decisions as to how to structure your code for better long-term maintainability and performance.

Web Components

In the Document Object Model (DOM), custom elements can be created and encapsulated by being attached to the DOM using Shadow DOM. Shadow DOM is a subtree of DOM elements that can be attached to the rendering document composed of a shadow host, shadow root, and shadow tree (see Figure 8-5).

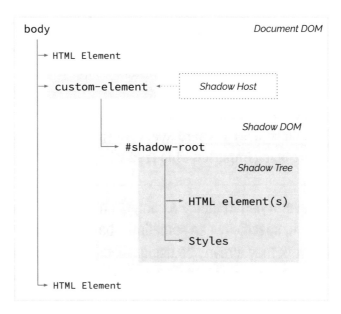

Figure 8-5. *Shadow DOM*

Components created using this technique are fully encapsulated, and the author has complete control as to what the consumer will be able to style vs. not because everything within the Shadow DOM is akin to a black box from the perspective of the parent page or component. For a short while, we were able to ignore the encapsulation by using shadow piercing combinators such as >>> or ::deep, but these have been deprecated or removed from most browsers in favor of the upcoming CSS Shadow Parts [6] specification currently being refined. Even after this new specification is implemented, however, the author of the component will still control what users will be able to fiddle with; specificity, !important, and shadow piercing combinations will continue to fail to edit styles that the component author did not open to being altered.

Architecturally speaking, the benefit of web components allows for styled web components that can be dropped into any UI without worry of being altered by the parent application's CSS. See Listings 8-8 to 8-11 and Figure 8-6.

Listing 8-8. Web Component HTML

```
<html lang="en">

<head>
  <title>Web Components</title>
  <link rel="stylesheet" href="./styles.css">
  <meta charset="utf-8">
</head>

<body>
  <h1>Components</h1>
  <p>Lorem ipsum dolor sit amet, consectetur adipiscing elit. Morbi sed
  neque semper ante mattis tempor. Morbi volutpat ex ante, eget vulputate
  ligula pulvinar gravida.</p>
  <p></p>
  <section class="components">
    <my-card title="Coffee">
      <slot name="content">
        <p>Aged cortado, carajillo saucer wings aftertaste...</p>
      </slot>
    </my-card>

    <my-card title="Cats" class="dark">
      <slot name="content">
        <p>Chew master's slippers I is not fat, I is fluffy...</p>
      </slot>
```

---

[6]https://drafts.csswg.org/css-shadow-parts/

```
    </my-card>
  </section>
  <div class="actions">
    <button type="button">More Components -></button>
  </div>
  <script src="./script.js"></script>
</body>

</html>
```

Listing 8-9. Web Component JavaScript (script.js)

```
const actionButtonEvent = new CustomEvent('actions', {
  bubbles: true,
  detail: { text: 'ok button' }
});

class MyCardComponent extends HTMLElement {
  constructor() {
    super();

    const shadow = this.attachShadow({ mode: 'open' });

    const card = document.createElement('div');
    card.setAttribute('class', 'card');

    const titleText = this.getAttribute('title');
    if (titleText) {
      const title = document.createElement('h2');
      title.innerText = titleText;
      card.appendChild(title);
    }

    const slot = document.createElement('slot');
    card.appendChild(slot);

    const actions = document.createElement('div');
    actions.setAttribute('class', 'actions');
    const button = document.createElement('button');
```

```
    button.innerText = 'OK';
    button.setAttribute('type', 'button');
    button.addEventListener('click', () => {
      this.dispatchEvent(actionButtonEvent);
    });
    actions.appendChild(button);
    card.appendChild(actions);

    const style = document.createElement('style');
    style.textContent = `@import './card.css'`;

    card.appendChild(style);
    shadow.appendChild(card);
  }
}

(function() {
  'use strict';
  customElements.define('my-card', MyCardComponent);
  document.querySelector('my-card').addEventListener('actions',
  e => console.log('outer actions event', e));
})();
```

Listing 8-10. Web Component CSS (card.css)

```
:host {
  font-family: sans-serif;
  --primary: mediumvioletred;
  --background: white;
  --text: #242529;
  --buttonText: white;
}
:host(.dark) {
  --background: #242529;
  --text: white;
}
```

```css
.card {
  background: var(--background);
  color: var(--text);
  box-shadow: 1px 1px 1px var(--primary), 0px 0px 2px lightgrey;
  padding: 1rem;
}

h2 { margin: 0 1rem 0 0; }

.actions {
  text-align: right;
  margin-top: 1rem;
}

button {
  background: var(--primary);
  color: var(--buttonText);
  font-family: sans-serif;
  padding: .5rem 1.5rem;
  border: none;
}
```

Listing 8-11. Web Component Page CSS (styles.css)

```css
html, body {
  background: #fafafa;
  padding: 36px;
  margin: 0;
}

section.components {
  display: flex;
  margin: 0 -1rem;
}

my-card { margin: 1rem; }

.actions { text-align: center; }
```

```
button {
  background: rgb(187, 255, 120);
  border: none;
  border-radius: 1rem;
  box-shadow: 1px 1px 1px 1px gray;
  margin-top: 2rem;
  padding: .5rem 3rem;
}

.dark {
  font-family: monospace;
  font-size: 1.0625rem;
}

p, h2 { font-variant: small-caps; }
```

Figure 8-6. *Web Component Output*

Notice how the button styles do not interact with each other even though styles are being applied directly to the button element in both style sheets. This is powerful because it means that components and applications can be built independently and used with each other without the fear of naming collisions. Some things do transfer through, however. The component, through the `:host` and lesser supported `:host-context` selectors, can have awareness of its context. In this case, the component is specifically looking to see whether its host has a class of dark. If it does, then it is styled differently. However, these are preplanned styles from the author. Should another class name be passed to this specific component, it would continue to display its defaults, seen on the left of Figure 8-7.

```
▼ <my-card title="Coffee"> event  custom…
   ▼ #shadow-root (open)
      ▼ <div class="card">
         <h2>Coffee</h2>
         ▼ <slot> contents
              <slot> ↵
            </slot>
         ▶ <div class="actions"> ··· </div>
            <style>@import './card.css'</style>
         </div>
      ▼ <slot name="content"> contents
         ▶ <p> ··· </p>
         </slot>
   </my-card>
```

Figure 8-7. *Node Tree Including Slots*

Some styles do bleed into the component. Elements in the slot or classes assigned directly to the host (the custom tag) are subject to both the component styles and page styles. Notice the paragraph tags in Figure 8-6; they take styles from both the parent and the component as described below.

Left component:

```
Browser default (serif) -> :host (sans-serif)
```

Right component:

```
Browser default (serif) -> :host (sans-serif) -> .dark (monospace)
```

`:host` is more specific than the browser defaults, and in turn, `.dark` is more specific than `:host`.

So why did the header also become monospace, when the buttons were unaffected? By adding a font-family of sans-serif to `.dark`, we essentially set monospace as the default font-family on the `:host`, that is as far as we can pierce into the component. The buttons have their own typeface specified inside the component CSS which is overriding the `:host` default and were therefore unaffected. Further attempts to reach into elements inside the component via specificity, such as doing `.dark button { ... }` even if no styles are set for that property, will not work.

The reason we were able to style the paragraph tags, and will continue to be able to do whatever we want with them, is because they are in a slot. The contents of the slot are actually being controlled by the parent. Looking at the DOM tree, one can see that the slot content lives outside of the shadow tree as seen in Figure 8-7.

The slot inside the shadow tree is nothing more than a placeholder. The content of the slot is in a sibling node of the `shadow-root`, and not in the `shadow-tree` itself. It is therefore not encapsulated like the rest of the component and can be styled like any other element on the page. Because it is a child of the host, however, styles assigned to the shadow host will cascade normally to those elements.

Styling Applications That Use Web Components

When creating an application that uses components, it is easy to start thinking only in terms of small reusable items and to lose sight of the greater picture. Consistency of typeface, colors, button styling, and so on across the application is something I think we can all agree is a good thing. However, if we are rewriting those styles in every component, we are setting ourselves up for discrepancies and a maintainability nightmare. How tightly encapsulated the components are affects the approach.

Regardless of encapsulation, however, starting with a file in which some reusable values are set to semantic, easily readable variables to be imported in all of the places helps in two ways: The same file is used everywhere, so consistency is gained, and because those values it contains are also being maintained in one place, should the primary brand color switch from blue to purple, one is not stuck looking for every instance of the color in the application. When using a precompiler such as Sass or Less, this is also a great place to set up some mixins. For more information about precompilers, see Chapter 7. Listing 8-12 shows an excerpt of what such a file might look like.

Listing 8-12. Sample Variable File

```
/* brand colors */
--primary: #8A4F7D;
--accent: #88A096;
--border-color: #DDDDDD;
--link-color: var(--accent);
--background: #FAFAFA;
--font-family: sans-serif;

--box-shadow: 1px 1px 1px var(--primary), 0px 0px 2px lightgrey;

/* breakpoints */
--small: 500px;
--medium: 800px;
--large: 1200px;

...
```

If the application still has a base style sheet whose styles are applied in and out of all components, it is a great place to put defaults such as what a link should look like and behave like on hover and focus, what headers should look like, and what are the application's base font and colors. This is a great place to set up your theme. (see Listing 8-13).

Listing 8-13. Sample Theme File

```
@import 'variable.css';

html, body {
  Background: var(--primary);
  padding: 0;
  margin: 0;
  font-family: var(--font-family);
  color: black
}

h1, h2, h3, h4, h5, h6 {
  color: var(--primary);
}
```

```
a:link,
a:visited {
  color: var(--accent);
}
a:hover,
a:focus {
  text-decoration: underline;
}
...
```

Once these two files are set up, components should only need to worry about layout and exceptions, things that are specific to that component and nothing else. A great gauge of a style or set of styles belonging in one of these files would be if you find yourself copying and pasting the same thing over and over again. If this is the case, it is time to consider whether these styles need to be imported or set as defaults somewhere.

If the components are tightly encapsulated and a theme file that cascades styling throughout the application is not possible, variables that can be imported become really critical. Importing an entire theme file into every component will just bloat the application because even though maintained in one place, it will essentially be copied in each component. Possibilities here include the use of preprocessors in order to create mixins, or breaking the theme file up into smaller chunks, buttons, tables, links, and so on so that only the needed portions get imported.

Summary

In this chapter we covered the common interaction mechanisms between CSS and JS to show how JS interacts with (and sometimes interferes with) our style sheets. We also looked at how the architecture of the libraries we use can affect how we structure our code. In the next chapter we will dive into various architectural best practices along with specific CSS architectural patterns, showing their strengths and weaknesses.

CHAPTER 9

Architectural Patterns

In order to produce an architectural approach for your CSS, it's important to clearly establish your goals and then settle on a general methodology. In this chapter we propose goals, guidelines, and methodologies for your consideration.

Approach

When working on web development, it's important to build a consistent approach that is sensitive to external factors and business demands. There are also considerations for our development team to be sure we can rapidly produce the desired results, and that the web site continues to look and work as expected as content is added and changed over time.

Note Since both *element* and *component* are technical words with a specific meaning in the context of the Web, we will use the word *widget* to refer to reusable building blocks made up of HTML+CSS.

While many frameworks will implement a widget with either a native or framework-based web component, this is neither a requirement nor a goal of good CSS architecture.

© Martine Dowden and Michael Dowden 2020
M. Dowden and M. Dowden, *Architecting CSS*, https://doi.org/10.1007/978-1-4842-5750-0_9

Goals

Referring back to Chapter 1, our goals are to achieve separation of concerns through high cohesion and low coupling. We want to minimize the cost of maintenance and overall development time while improving the developer experience. Taking these high-level goals as a starting point, we can recommend the following concrete objectives for our HTML and CSS:

- We should be able to design a modularized widget with HTML and CSS that stands on its own without depending on external CSS.

- When we drop a widget into our web site, we want it to take on the overall look and feel of our site and brand.

- It shouldn't be necessary to artificially boost specificity or precedence (such as by adding an ID selector or `!important` annotation) to style a widget as intended.

- General content edits in an HTML document (inserting images, adding paragraphs, adjusting rows/columns in a table, adding items to a list, etc.) should not necessitate updates to the style sheets.

- It should be easy for someone new to join our team and figure out how to make adjustments to the design of our pages and widgets.

- Our styles should be easy to read, understand, and troubleshoot.

- The design of our web sites should be easy to re-theme without impacting the layout and functionality of the site.

- It should be straightforward to make design changes (such as colors and typography) without needing to use search-and-replace on the CSS properties across our style sheets.

- We should be able to adjust the styles of Widget-A and Widget-B independently, without worrying about changes to one impacting the other unintentionally.

- User's wishes with regard to style should be respected to improve their experience and overall accessibility.

In his 2012 blog post about CSS architecture,[1] Philip Walton issued an important reminder: "stripping [sic] all presentational code from your HTML doesn't fulfill the goal if your CSS requires an intimate knowledge of your HTML structure in order to work."

Guidelines

Working from the earlier listed goals, there are a few general guidelines we can derive that may prove helpful in selecting the right methodology. These aren't hard-and-fast rules, but a reasonable set of default positions you may choose to work from.

- Avoid class names that mirror the name of the tag they are on, attribute values, or pseudo classes (e.g., no more `<button type="button" class="button">` or `<input type="password" class="password">`).

- Avoid generic class names such as `content`, `container`, `wrapper`, `right`, and `left`. These names don't provide any meaningful understanding as to their usage or intent, and they are subject to naming collisions with other style sheets on our project or with third-party libraries.

- Generally, avoid using IDs as selectors.

- Prefer selector specificities between [0 1 0] and [0 2 2]. Any lower and you run the risk of leaking styles into the rest of your site. Any higher and you risk overwriting inheritance or making a value unintentionally sticky. Higher specificities also risk being overly verbose and either brittle or difficult to understand. Use higher specificity selectors with purpose and care.

- Avoid using `!important` in your style sheets and inline styles in your HTML.

- Optimize your CSS architectural decisions for the developer experience, and the ease and accuracy of ongoing changes, rather than becoming overly concerned with performance of the style sheets.

---

[1] https://philipwalton.com/articles/css-architecture/

- Choose a consistent naming strategy.

- Separate concerns.

- Use child and sibling selectors only when necessary (ideally just within a widget), but avoid the use of descendant selectors as they have an unknown amount of impact.

Methodologies

For most things in code, there is more than one way to approach any given problem. CSS architecture is no different. There are four patterns that stand out among the rest when considering how to structure one's code and name one's classes: BEM, OOCSS, SMACSS, and ITCSS as listed in Table 9-1. We will discuss each of these in the following text, highlighting some of their strengths and weaknesses.

Table 9-1. *CSS Methodologies*

Year	Creator	Methodology: Official Web Site
2008	Nicole Sullivan	OOCSS: `https://github.com/stubbornella/oocss/wiki`
2009	Yandex	BEM[2]: `https://en.bem.info/methodology/`
2012	Jonathan Snook	SMACSS: `http://smacss.com/`
2015	Harry Roberts	ITCSS[3]: `https://itcss.io/`

One thing the following methodologies have in common is the heavy use of classes in both the HTML and CSS. They all agree on one specific point – the only use classes serve in the HTML is for CSS or JavaScript binding.

It is important to point out that many CSS professionals mix and match their favorite parts of each of these methodologies. As always, choose what works for you and your team, but be consistent about it.

---

[2]Gallagher did not create BEM, but popularized a simplified syntax for CSS based upon BEM.
[3]`www.creativebloq.com/web-design/manage-large-scale-web-projects-new-css-architecture-itcss-41514731`

OOCSS

Originally presented by Nicole Sullivan at Web Directions North, Object-Oriented CSS (OOCSS) borrows concepts from Object-Oriented Design in order to provide structure to CSS. The Object in OOCSS is what we have been calling a widget and is defined by Sullivan as "a repeating visual pattern, that can be abstracted into an independent snippet of HTML, CSS, and possibly JavaScript. That object can then be reused throughout a site."[4]

There are two core rules of OOCSS that aim to produce flexible, modular, and swappable widgets. They are

- Separate structure from skin

- Separate container from content

These rules will be illustrated using the HTML in Listing 9-1.

Listing 9-1. OOCSS Example HTML

```
<body>
  <div class="sidebar theme-light">
    <nav>
      <ul>
        <li><a href="/home">Home</a></li>
        <li><a href="/about">About</a></li>
      </ul>
    </nav>
    <form class="login">
      <input type="text" placeholder="Username">
      <input type="password" placeholder="Password">
      <button type="submit">Login</button>
    </form>
  </div>
```

---

[4]https://github.com/stubbornella/oocss/wiki

```
<main>
  <section class="hero theme-light">
    <p>Lorem ipsum dolor sit amet...<p>
    <button class="call-to-action">Subscribe</button>
  </section>
</main>
</body>
```

Separate Structure from Skin

Structure (or layout) refers to the location of elements on the page, or the function and interaction of those elements. Layout properties include those items that impact size and position of elements, such as height, width, margin, padding, and overflow.

Skin (or theme) refers to the visual aspect of the elements. Theme properties include color, border, box-shadow, font, and opacity, among others.

The structure and skin should be applied through different classes as shown in Listing 9-2.

Listing 9-2. OOCSS Separate Structure from Skin

```
/* OOCSS wants this */
.theme-light {
  color: slategray;
  background-color: lightgoldenrodyellow;
  border: 1px solid navy;
}
.sidebar {
  padding: 1rem;
  float: left;
  width: 200px;
}
.hero {
  margin: 1rem 1rem 1rem 250px;
  padding: 1rem;
}
```

```
/* Not this */
.sidebar {
  color: slategray;
  background-color: lightgoldenrodyellow;
  border: 1px solid navy;
  padding: 1rem;
  float: left;
  width: 200px;
}
.hero {
  color: slategray;
  background-color: lightgoldenrodyellow;
  border: 1px solid navy;
  margin: 1rem 1rem 1rem 250px;
  padding: 1rem;
}
```

This approach allows theming to be applied to a wide range of elements and maintained in just a single location. In order to implement OOCSS as intended, it will be necessary to add classes to the HTML to avoid relying solely on the semantics of the HTML.

Separate Container from Content

This basically means to prefer styling based upon attributes rather than location. So given the HTML in Listing 9-1, we have the CSS shown in Listing 9-3.

Listing 9-3. OOCSS Separate Container from Content

```
/* Given this default */
button {
  background-color: lightblue;
}

/* OOCSS wants you to do this */
.call-to-action {
  background-color: lightgreen;
}
```

```
/* Not this */
.hero button {
  background-color: lightgreen;
}
```

There are several purposes for this recommendation such as better consistency and maintainability. Some specific goals:

- Buttons look the same regardless of location, unless the HTML specifies something else via class.

- All elements with the `call-to-action` class will have the same look, regardless of tag or location.

- Looking at the HTML for the button, I can easily find its ruleset.

- Avoids artificially inflating the specificity allowing styles to be predictably overridden when necessary.

While these are general guidelines without providing too many specifics, there are no apparent problems with following these recommendations.

However, do keep in mind that CSS requires every property to have a value, so any values not provided will use defaults. Also different elements (say, `<a>` and `<button>`) have different default values for these properties and a different default appearance. So when using an approach like OOCSS and leaning on class selectors without an accompanying type selector, consider what might happen when this class is applied to a new element with different defaults.

BEM

BEM stands for Block, Element, Modifier, which summarizes the naming convention used and overall approach to organization. The "Block" in BEM refers to our concept of the reusable widget. The use of "Block" and "Element" in BEM is unfortunate as the naming overlaps similar, but not identical, HTML concepts with those same names. (To avoid confusion we'll use the BEM concepts in *italics* within this chapter.)

While BEM is a full-blown front-end methodology, it is the naming convention that has become most popular among CSS developers. The naming follows this pattern:

```
block__element--modifier
```

The use of two underscores and hyphens between naming is so that a single hyphen can be used within a section name, such as

```
login-form__password-field--visible
```

One common question in BEM is how to decide if a given item should be a *block* or an *element*. The general guideline is that if the section of code cannot be used separately from its parent container, then it's an *element*. If it can be reused independently, then it's a *block*.[5]

The HTML in Listing 9-4 shows an example of BEM naming using the same basic HTML structure as our OOCSS example.

Listing 9-4. BEM Example HTML

```
<body>
  <div class="sidebar sidebar--theme-light">
    <!-- Mix: both an element and a block -->
    <nav class="sidebar__nav nav">
      <ul>
        <li class="nav__item"><a href="/home">Home</a></li>
        <li class="nav__item">
          <a href="/about">About</a>
        </li>
      </ul>
    </nav>
    <form class="login-form">
      <input type="text" placeholder="Username">
      <input
        type="password"
        class="login-form__password-field--visible"
        placeholder="Password">
      <button
        class="login-form__submit"
        type="submit">Login</button>
    </form>
  </div>
```

---

[5]https://en.bem.info/methodology/quick-start/#should-i-create-a-block-or-an-element

```
  <main>
    <section class="hero hero--theme-light">
      <p>Lorem ipsum dolor sit amet...<p>
      <button
        class="hero__call-to-action">Subscribe</button>
    </section>
  </main>
</body>
```

In many cases you may see Nicolas Gallagher's simplified BEM naming convention[6] referenced, which looks something like this:

```
ComponentName-descendent--modifier
```

As you may have noticed, this notation replaces hyphenated section names with camel case and uses a better naming convention that doesn't overlap with HTML. Updating our HTML example may give something like the code in Listing 9-5.

Listing 9-5. Simplified BEM HTML

```
<body>
  <div class="Sidebar Sidebar--themeLight">
    <!-- Mix: both an element and a block -->
    <nav class="Sidebar-nav Nav">
      <ul>
        <li class="Nav-item"><a href="/home">Home</a></li>
        <li class="Nav-item">
          <a href="/about">About</a>
        </li>
      </ul>
    </nav>
    <form class="LoginForm">
      <input type="text" placeholder="Username">
      <input
```

---

[6]http://nicolasgallagher.com/about-html-semantics-front-end-architecture/

```
      type="password"
      class="LoginForm-passwordField--visible"
      placeholder="Password">
    <button
      class="LoginForm-submit"
      type="submit">Login</button>
  </form>
</div>
<main>
  <section class="Hero Hero--themeLight">
    <p>Lorem ipsum dolor sit amet...<p>
    <button class="Hero-callToAction">Subscribe</button>
  </section>
</main>
</body>
```

One goal of BEM is to flatten the structure inside of a *block* so that the related CSS doesn't necessarily have to change if the nesting of the HTML changes. In the example from Listing 9-4, we could change from using <ul> and <li> tags to using <div> tags for the nav__item and the CSS would not need to change. As this illustrates, BEM discourages using HTML elements as CSS selectors.

Another goal of BEM is predictable and consistent naming and simple maintainability. For instance, it should be very easy to perform a text search on a project to find everywhere a given class name is used, making it possible to remove unused rules from our style sheets with confidence.

One benefit of BEM is that the style sheet can be very easily broken into multiple files with a high degree of confidence, based upon *block*.

The use of modifiers in BEM contradicts the recommendation of OOCSS to create general-purpose and reusable styles that represent the skin or theme. This can be at least partially overcome using SCSS mixins, but is a difference worth noting. While it makes BEM very predictable, it greatly reduces the ability to compose reusable styles in favor of being very explicit.

SMACSS

Scalable and Modular Architecture for CSS (SMACSS) is a CSS methodology and a book[7] of the same name, both by Jonathan Snook. At its core SMACSS is a categorization system for rulesets. There are five categories:

- **Base** – The base rules establish the defaults. Each rule should generally apply to just one element. This is a great place for normalization and base font size.

- **Layout** – This is where we put the dimensional and positioning declarations, along with any glue we may need for our widgets to work together.

- **Module** – These are where we find the reusable widgets in SMACSS. These modular design units such as callouts, sidebars, and login forms are defined here.

- **State** – Most web applications reveal a large amount of state visually within the design components, which belong here. This may include such values as visible/hidden, active/inactive, hover, focus, and expanded/collapsed.

- **Theme** – Declarations that impact the look, feel, and brand (but not the layout or functionality) are generally thematic. This is similar to the skin concept from OOCSS.

The purpose of categorizing things is not to create artificial barriers, but to better codify repeating patterns within the design.[8] SMACSS does not penalize exceptions to the categorization guidelines, but simply recommends that exceptions be justified as advantageous.

Class Naming

Rules in the *base* category typically do not use classes and have no need for a naming convention. For layout rules, use an `l-` prefix (lowercase "L" followed by a hyphen) on class names, such as `.l-leftnav`. For state rules, use an `is-` prefix such as `.is-visible`. These rules are shown in Listing 9-6 to illustrate how they fit within the HTML document.

---

[7]`http://smacss.com/book/`

[8]`http://smacss.com/book/categorizing`

Listing 9-6. SMACSS Naming

```
<body class="l-leftnav">
  <div id="sidebar" class="sidebar-left">
    <!-- Mix: both an element and a block -->
    <nav class="nav">
      <ul class="l-stacked">
        <li><a href="/home">Home</a></li>
        <li><a href="/about">About</a></li>
      </ul>
    </nav>
    <form class="login">
      <input type="text" placeholder="Username">
      <input
        type="password"
        class="is-visible password"
        placeholder="Password">
      <button type="submit">Login</button>
    </form>
  </div>
  <main>
    <section class="hero hero-light">
      <p>Lorem ipsum dolor sit amet...<p>
      <button class="call-to-action">Subscribe</button>
    </section>
  </main>
</body>
```

As you can see in Listing 9-6, modules (widgets) simply have a meaningful name. We can further clarify modules by "subclassing" which adds a new section to the name, similar to a *modifier* in BEM. For example, .hero-light would be a subclass of .hero. Listing 9-7 shows how the naming convention can be used within a style sheet.

Listing 9-7. SMACSS Example CSS

```
/* SMACSS wants you to do this */
.l-leftnav #sidebar { ... }
.login input[type=password] { ... }
```

217

```
.l-stacked > * { ... }
.hero { height: 8rem; border: 2px solid green; }
.hero-light { border-color: lightgreen; }

/* Not this */
#sidebar.sidebar-left { ... }
.login .password { ... }
.l-leftnav .nav li { ... }
.hero { height: 8rem; border: 2px solid green; }
.hero.hero-light {
  height: 8rem;
  border: 2px solid lightgreen;
}
```

Recommendations

There are two overarching goals to the SMACSS recommendations:

1. **Improve semantics** – This means making it easier for developers to understand how and why widgets and elements are being used.

2. **Increase orthogonality** – In the SMACSS book, Snook states the goal as "Decrease reliance on specific HTML,"[9] which simply means restructuring of HTML should have minimal impact on our CSS.

There are a few guidelines that the methodology recommends based upon these goals:

- Trigger layout-specific changes based upon a layout class, not a page name.

- Use module (widget) class names instead of HTML elements in selectors.

- Avoid setting thematic defaults on common elements such as input fields, buttons, and tables.

As you've probably noticed, these recommendations closely mirror those we established at the beginning of the chapter, which were derived from our exploration of software architecture in Chapter 1.

---

[9]http://smacss.com/book/html5

ITCSS

Created by Harry Roberts, Inverted Triangle CSS (ITCSS) attempts to address selector specificity using the natural priority of CSS. The style sheets are relegated into layers[10] based upon their purpose very differently from OOCSS and SMACSS, as shown in Figure 9-1.

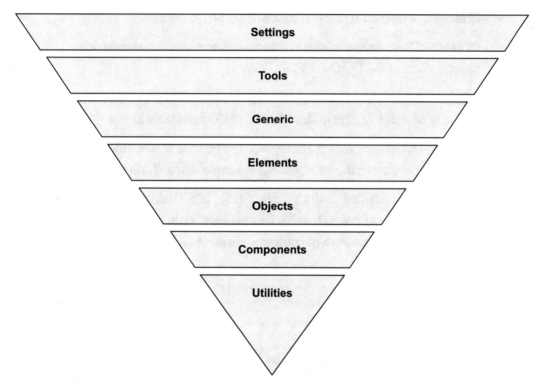

Figure 9-1. *ITCSS Diagram*

The base of the triangle (at the top of the diagram) represents the broadest and least specific rules, with the most explicit rules near the point of the triangle. These layers are further defined as follows:

- **Settings** – Intended for preprocessors, this layer includes variable definitions and site-wide settings such as font and colors. Should generally not output any CSS.

---

[10]www.xfive.co/blog/itcss-scalable-maintainable-css-architecture/

- **Tools** – Global mixins and functions for further reuse. This is primarily intended for preprocessors and should generally avoid outputting CSS.

- **Generic** – Normalization and reset of styles, CSS variables, and box-sizing settings. From this layout on should produce CSS. This is similar to the base rules category in SMACSS.

- **Elements** – Default styles for standard HTML elements.

- **Objects** – Class-based selectors which define reusable framework objects such as the OOCSS Media Object.

- **Components** – This is where our widgets come into play and the majority of styles will be in the Objects or Components layers.

- **Utilities** – Helper classes that may need to be able to override everything earlier in the triangle. For example, show/hide classes.

Rather than defining naming or design practices, ITCSS recommends a specific structure and organization of the style rules themselves, without providing too much detail around what sorts of rules are permitted.[11] As such ITCSS is fully compatible with OOCSS, SMACSS, and BEM.

Processes

One of the important roles a software architect often fills is to help establish good processes and practices for their team. It's important that your processes fit into the larger framework of web site publishing and delivery.

Imagine you are building a web site that pulls content from a Content Management System (CMS) which is managed by the company's marketing team. While it may be possible to modify the output produced by the CMS or to train the marketing team to add classes to certain elements, this may put too much pressure on the content team. It may be more reliable to simply write CSS that achieves the desired results with the content you receive. In this example the web development team has control over some of the HTML, but not all of it.

---

[11]www.creativebloq.com/web-design/manage-large-scale-web-projects-new-css-architecture-itcss-41514731

Decision Making

Often there will be two or more approaches that can be used to fulfill a goal, and it will be up to you to compare these options and make a decision. Your methodology of choice will likely be the first such decision, but Listing 9-8 illustrates some code decisions based upon the question, "How do we highlight the password in red on error?"

Listing 9-8. CSS Reuse Dilemma

```
/* CSS Rulesets */
.red-border: { border: 2px solid red; }
.password: { color: black; }

<!-- Sample HTML -->
<form class="login">
  <input type="text" placeholder="Username">
  <input type="password" placeholder="Password">
  <button type="submit">Login</button>
</form>

/*** How do we highlight the password in red on error? ***/

/* OPTION 1 - Add CSS Selector */
.login [type=password]:invalid,
.red-border: {
  border: 2px solid red;
}
.password: { color: black; }

/* OPTION 2 - Use SCSS Mixin */
.login [type=password]:invalid { .red-border; }

<!-- OPTION 3 - Add class to HTML -->
<input
  class="red-border"
  type="password"
  placeholder="Password">
```

The example in Listing 9-8 shows three options to code reuse based upon state, but Listing 9-9 shows two different ways to set the default font on a page.

Listing 9-9. Set Default Font

```css
/* Cascade from the <body> tag */
body { font-family: helvetica, arial, sans-serif; }
p { font-family: 'Lucida Handwriting', cursive; }

/* Set explicitly on every element */
* { font-family: Consolas, 'Liberation Mono', monospace; }
p, p * {
  font-family: 'Lucida Handwriting', cursive;
}
```

Most style sheet authors choose to cascade font default from the body tag as shown in Listing 9-9 rather than using the universal selector; however, both are technically possible. Because the universal selector has a specificity of zero, any rule will override it; however, since it's set on every single element, simply resetting the font on a the <p> element will *not* change the font for any child elements such as anchor tags, definitions, buttons, labels, and so on. To achieve this behavior (which is the default when depending on inheritance from body), we need to either apply the change to each subelement individually or use the universal selector again.

Note   Class names only provide meaning to page authors and developers. Your choice of class names should reflect this. Your class names do not convey any meaning whatsoever to user agents or systems and are never displayed to the human visitors to your pages.[12]

More than likely, whatever approach you choose, your style sheets will not satisfy all of the goals stated at the beginning of the chapter. You'll need to decide which goals are most important for your team and situation. Some specific questions you may need to ask include

- How big is your project/how big will it get (widgets, files, etc.)?

- How big is your team/how big do you expect to grow?

---

[12]http://nicolasgallagher.com/about-html-semantics-front-end-architecture/

- Do you need to support interchangeable themes?

- Do your developers have more control over the HTML or the CSS (many applications involve pulling content, data, or styles from external sources)?

Linting

One way to help ensure cross-browser compatibility, accessibility, and generally good code is via linting. Linters are tools that check syntax and formatting for errors. Depending on the tool used, some will also check for inefficiencies or problematic patterns. The W3 has a validation service[13] but many prefer to validate code as they go. Tools such as CSS Lint can be run in the browser[14] via command line[15] or even as editor extensions.[16]

Precompiled CSS, such as Sass or Less, will not compile if not valid, so linting is much less of an issue. However, linters do exist for precompiled CSS languages and can prove very helpful in debugging and in flagging potentially problematic rule combinations and redundancy.

Testing

Like most code, CSS can be tested. There are a number of libraries available to do just that. There are two main ways that CSS can be tested: via unit tests or snapshots.

Unit Testing

Unit testing CSS involves checking that styles that are expected to be applied are in fact set on the element. Libraries such as Quixote[17] test that what is being rendered in the browser is what the author intends. The author can select a specific element by class or ID and verify any CSS property.

---

[13]https://jigsaw.w3.org/css-validator/validator
[14]http://csslint.net/#results
[15]https://github.com/CSSLint/csslint/wiki/Command-line-interface
[16]https://github.com/CSSLint/csslint/wiki/IDE-integration
[17]https://github.com/jamesshore/quixote

When using precompilers, mixins can also be tested. Similar to functions, mixins have inputs and outputs; therefore, outputs can be tested based on input passed. Libraries such as Barista[18] or True[19] can make sure that mixin outputs match the author's intent.

Visual Regression Testing

The other way to test CSS is through visual regression testing. Libraries such as Cypress[20] or Jest[21] provide a framework to take and compare snapshots. By checking current snapshots against the reference ones, developers can be notified of unintended side effects when CSS is changed. Any nonmatching snapshots will raise a flag for the author to check on.

Code Review

While linting and automated testing are a fantastic way to validate your CSS in a predictable way, there is a limit to how much of your CSS architecture can be validated with automation. Meaningful code reviews can be a great way to verify

- Consistency in implementation
- That architectural decisions are being followed
- Minimal code repetition

Furthermore, code reviews are an opportunity to have open discussions about architectural decisions and specific consequences of those decisions. Code reviews should never be used as a way to judge other developers, but as a forum for sharing knowledge, learning from each other, and ensuring the long-term success of your team and project.

---

[18]https://developer.helpscout.com/seed/css-unit-testing/
[19]https://github.com/oddbird/true
[20]https://docs.cypress.io/guides/tooling/visual-testing.html#Functional-vs-visual-testing
[21]https://jestjs.io/docs/en/snapshot-testing

Summary

In this chapter you have learned about the architectural patterns we can use to build our style sheets using everything CSS has to offer. Specifically, we discussed

- Goals and guidelines that can help assess various options

- The CSS methodologies OOCSS, BEM, SMACSS, and ITCSS

- Processes you can use to evaluate your decisions to stay on track

Now you're ready to select and implement a CSS architecture methodology on your own projects! Best of luck, and happy coding!

Index

A

Andrew, Rachel, 25
Animation
    keyframe, 151, 153–157
    performance, 163
    property values, 154, 155
Apparao, Vidur, 21
Architectural approach, 205
    goals, 206
    guidelines, 207, 208
Architecture
    software, 4
    web, 11
At-rules, 14
    @import, 55
    @media (*see* Media query)
    @supports, 4, 56 (*see also* Fallbacks)
attr() function, 54
Attribute selector, 31

B

Block, Element, Modifier (BEM), 212–215
blur() function, 51
Boland, Tim, 23
Border-box
    element, 86
    padding, 84
Bos, Bert, 20
Box model, 73

Box-sizing, 74
    border-box (*see* Border-box)
    content-box (*see* Content-box)
    margin collapse, 78, 79
Browser, *see* User agent
btn-warning class, 190
Bug-prone layout, 102

C

calc() function, 52
Cascading
    properties, 70
    value processing, 71, 72
Cascading Style Sheets (CSS)
    architecture, 208
    declarations, 3, 4
    definition, 1
    history, 20–27
    language features, 3
    property, 4
    structure, 3, 4
    Turing complete, 2
Class selectors, 29
Cohesion, 6
Color functions, 169, 171
Combinators, 35–37
Component-based
    architecture, 186
Content-box
    in code, 76

Printed in the United States
By Bookmasters